LIVING WITH
ADHD

LIVING WITH
ADHD

• • •

Simple Exercises to
Change Your Daily Life

THOM HARTMANN

Healing Arts Press
Rochester, Vermont

Healing Arts Press
One Park Street
Rochester, Vermont 05767
www.HealingArtsPress.com

Healing Arts Press is a division of Inner Traditions International

First edition published in 1998 by Underwood Books under the title *Healing ADD: Simple Exercises That Will Change Your Daily Life*
Second revised and updated edition published in 2020 by Healing Arts Press

Note to the reader: *This book is intended as an informational guide. The remedies, approaches, and techniques described herein are meant to supplement, and not to be a substitute for, professional medical care or treatment. They should not be used to treat a serious ailment without prior consultation with a qualified health care professional.*

Cataloging-in-Publication Data for this title is available from the Library of Congress

ISBN 978-1-62055-900-0 (print)
ISBN 978-1-62055-901-7 (ebook)

Printed and bound in the United States

10 9 8 7 6 5 4 3 2

Text design and layout by Priscilla Baker
This book was typeset in Garamond Premier Pro with Futura, Gill Sans, and Trenda used as display typefaces

To send correspondence to the author of this book, mail a first-class letter to the author c/o Inner Traditions • Bear & Company, One Park Street, Rochester, VT 05767, and we will forward the communication, or contact the author directly at **www.thomhartmann.com.**

Progress is the injustice each generation commits with regard to its predecessors.

E. M. CIORAN (1911–1995),
ROMANIAN-BORN FRENCH PHILOSOPHER,
THE TROUBLE WITH BEING BORN, 1973

Contents

Foreword by Richard Bandler   ix

Acknowledgments   xi

The First Step to Healing   1

PART 1
Reframing ADHD and Why Doing So Matters

1. How We Each Experience the World Differently   4

2. When Is a "Difference" a "Disease"?   11

3. Life Is What We Think It Is   33

4. What Is ADHD?   46

5. How People Are Damaged by Growing Up with ADHD   54

PART 2
Living with ADHD in the Modern World

6. The Beginning of Stigmatization of ADHD   62

7. ADHD as a Response to the Modern World   67

8. If You Have ADHD, Society Needs You   71

PART 3
·····
Healing Memories of a Lifetime with ADHD

9. What Doesn't Kill Us Makes Us Stronger   76

10. Finding Your Calm and Powerful Center   79

11. Reconstructing the Past   92

12. Shedding Fears and Phobias   100

PART 4
·····
Specific Strategies to Heal "ADHD Dysfunctions"

13. Reorganizing Your Timelines   108

14. Becoming Multimodally Functional   117

15. Building New Motivation Strategies   123

16. Anchoring Positive States for Future Access   132

17. Acquiring New Learning Skills   139

18. Learning New Communication Skills   143

PART 5
·····
Reinventing Your Life

19. Making Intentional Decisions
    about Friendships   156

20. Discover Your Purpose
    ADHD Can Be Your Greatest Gift   159

21. Re-create Your Environment Intentionally   167

· ● ·

Bibliography   171

Index   173

Foreword

Richard Bandler

IT'S ABOUT TIME somebody started to look at what's considered pathological with new eyes so that we can all see that being different doesn't necessarily mean that something is wrong with you.

You can take the qualities and characteristics, especially of children—whether they're supposed to be hyperactive or have a deficit, disorder, or whatever it may be called—and look at it in a nonpathological way. In this and his other books, Thom Hartmann points out how these behaviors were assets in the past—and how they can be in the present and future as well. He suggests ways that we can begin to look at what's supposedly wrong with our children and ourselves and instead see what's missing in our educational system, what's missing in the skills that are taught to psychotherapists, and what's missing in the things we teach our doctors.

Using the techniques in this book, professionals and non-professionals alike can become agents of change and agents of learning. You can learn to use the skills and abilities that come with your genetic structure to transform your life in positive and constructive ways.

Everybody is genetically different in one way or another, but it doesn't have to mean you can't function in the society that we have.

Thom's conceptualization of the ADHD syndrome is refreshing. In a very real sense, we all are a syndrome—"syndrome" is really nothing more than a metaphor itself. The fact is that there is nothing wrong with most of us that a good, clean change of attitude and some new skills wouldn't fix.

I hope that as you read this book thoroughly, it sinks into your mind that these historical perspectives, and the capacity for transformation, are true about you, whether you have ADHD or not.

RICHARD BANDLER is the cofounder of Neuro-Linguistic Programming (NLP). He conducts workshops and training seminars internationally and continues to develop new strategies to improve the lives of people around the world.

Acknowledgments

LIVING WITH ADHD IS A BOOK about healing from the damage done to a person by growing up as a "Hunter in a Farmer's world," and about learning new ways to see and do things so that what our culture calls ADHD is not so much of a problem in one's life.

Much of the theoretical and practical content of this book is grounded in the technology of Neuro-Linguistic Programming (NLP), which was first codified over forty years ago by Richard Bandler and John Grinder. Numerous excellent books and courses are available on NLP, and more information is available from The Society of NLP, PO Box 828, Hopatcong, NJ 07843, and on Richard Bandler's website. I am personally indebted to Leif Roland, Tamara Andreas, Michael Breen, Paul McKenna, and, particularly, Richard Bandler for being my real-world in-person trainers in various aspects of NLP. I also respect and thank John Grinder, John La Valle, Rex Steven Sikes, Connierae and Steve Andreas, Robert Dilts, Sidney Rosen, and Jerry Mander for what they have taught me in a less personal (but nonetheless effective) fashion through their writings, tapes, and other publications.

The identities of all clients in this book have been altered to protect their privacy, and some reconstructed conversations have been abbreviated or otherwise modified for the sake of brevity and clarity.

Thanks also go to my agent, Bill Gladstone, and Ehud Sperling, Jon Graham, Jeanie Levitan, Patricia Rydle, Kayla Toher, and the design team at Inner Traditions, who did such a great job bringing this book back into print in a new and improved format.

And special thanks are due to my wife, Louise Hartmann, for providing wise counsel and a writer-supportive environment during the creation of this work.

NLP is a trademark registered in the United Kingdom by Richard Bandler. In all cases, use of NLP in this book is meant to acknowledge that and any other trademarks.

• ● •

Men are born ignorant, not stupid; they are made stupid by education.

BERTRAND RUSSELL (1872–1970),
BRITISH PHILOSOPHER AND
MATHEMATICIAN SUMMARIZING HELVÉTIUS,
A HISTORY OF WESTERN PHILOSOPHY, 1945

The First Step to Healing

ODDS ARE YOU'RE READING this book because you have a child with ADD or ADHD, your spouse has it, you have it yourself, or some combination of these situations apply to your life. In any of these cases, the first step to healing or helping others heal is to see them and yourself in a new way—a way that allows for change, offers hope, *and* provides specific and useful tools. That's the goal of this book.

Back in the old days, when they milled grain between two huge, round, moving stones, it was common to throw some sand in with the grain as it was poured between the stones. The purpose of this sand was to break up the grain, providing it with a rough, hard surface between the millstones so that the grinding process was more rapid, complete, thorough, and uniform. This sand was referred to as *grist*.

This book is written in a new language: every word means exactly what it says. Many words also have secondary or tertiary meanings. If you feel a little confused, this is a normal reaction; confusion is one of the first and most primary tools of Neuro-Linguistic Programming.

There is considerable discussion in the first half of this book about the nature of reality and the definition of "normal." While to the "normal" reader, this may seem overlong, experience tells me that the ADHD reader will find this among the most liberating and healing parts of the book.

Some of the apparently strong statements of opinion on political or social matters are here to provoke the reader into an encounter with internal mental resistance. When you experience statements that you find offensive, contradictory, or possibly even unbelievable, simply look up and to the right and say to yourself, "Oh, that must be one of those rants he told me to look for."

Unless you want to, you don't need to let the content of the rant percolate into your brain; indeed, feel free to not agree with all of it, and not even try to not think about ways it may not be—or may be—true or applicable. But do notice how it affects you. This is the grist for *your* mill of personal transformation, and it provides you with the solid, grounded place from which you can help your child or significant other transform their lives.

PART I

Reframing ADHD and Why Doing So Matters

1

How We Each Experience the World Differently

What a terrible thing to have lost one's mind. Or not to have a mind at all. How true that is.

DAN QUAYLE, AMERICAN VICE PRESIDENT, MISQUOTING THE UNITED NEGRO COLLEGE FUND'S SLOGAN "A MIND IS A TERRIBLE THING TO WASTE," 1989

ADHD IS ABOUT THE DIFFERENCES among humans. We and our children have different hair, eyes, and body sizes and different preferences in a thousand areas. Some of us prefer high levels of stimulation, while others like a more quiet world. Some are attracted to novelty and variety, whereas others are most comfortable with the consistent and predictable. In these and many other ways, we aggregate differences that sometimes collect in such a way that we put a label on them, such as "ADHD."

There are other, more fundamental differences between people, however. At the level of these differences, it's possible to gain direct access into the way a person's mind works, the way they store and process experience and emotion, and the way they make decisions. These differences have to do with how we experience the world around us.

The exercises and examples in this book present ways to work with and around ADHD and heal from the damage done by a world that doesn't understand the Hunter in a Farmer's World (or, in other words, people with ADHD living in a world unsuited to their way of being in the world). Most of the exercises are grounded in a system called Neuro-Linguistic Programming, or NLP. It's a wide-ranging, comprehensive system first developed over fifty years ago by Richard Bandler and John Grinder that has, over the decades, had a huge influence (albeit rarely acknowledged) in a variety of fields, particularly in psychotherapy, psychology, and advertising and communications. NLP, in a nutshell, is a toolkit of ways to better communicate, better understand others' communications, and reconfigure our own understandings and experiences of the world in a way that is therapeutic or useful.

Later in the book, after we go over foundational concepts of what "reality" is and how our thinking defines our world, we'll go into detail about what NLP calls *Representational Systems*. For now, consider them the primary senses—sight, sound, feeling, taste, and smell—through which the world enters our and our children's minds.

Many people are shocked when they first discover that not everybody sees (or hears or feels) the world the same way they do. It's a fact, however, that we each have our own particular ways of experiencing life, and most people have a single representational system upon which they most heavily rely. We'll go into this, and the consequences of it, in more detail in later chapters. We'll also discover how knowing a person's primary representational system is a vital bit of information if you want to work with, help heal, or even communicate with that person.

It also raises another question, Why do we (or our kids) choose the friends we do, and what can we do with that knowledge?

While this has been the subject of endless speculation since the times of Plato and Proverbs, I've not seen a definitive study on it anywhere. Some people choose their friends because of geographic proximity or shared interest—many people have made friends with the person next door, a coworker, or fellow hobbyist. There may even be elements of shared ethnicity, intelligence, or temperament. But that alone can't account for why we feel drawn to one person and not another.

Another possibility is that it has to do with shared representational systems. Visual people feel most comfortable with other visual people, since they have a shared view of reality. Two kinesthetic people share an experience of the world, and two primarily auditory persons would have similar understandings of what life is telling them.

Yet people who have a different perception of the world from ours have interesting and often valuable lessons to teach us. Particularly when we understand our differences, other people's perspectives can help us expand our experience of life in ways that may not otherwise have been available to us.

Check out this simple test, and give it to a few friends, your family, and your children. The results will open a window to—or tell you more about, or give you a better feel for, depending on your preferred representational system—yourself and those close to you. It'll also introduce you to a core concept of NLP: people experience the world differently from each other, which is sometimes stated as, "The map is not the territory." After you've taken the test and compared your results with a few friends, consider which of these possibilities may be at work in your relationships.

And if this small revelation is useful for you, continue reading, because this is only the surface-most level of the technology of change that can lead to healing ADHD.

THE HARTMANN MODALITY-PREFERENCE MEASUREMENT INDEX

Rank each of the three answer options below between one and three, with three being "most often true" and one "least often true." When you're finished, add up all the As, Bs, and Cs. The numerical scores will tell you (Show you? Give you a feeling for?) which of the three representational systems you're most and least comfortable with. Keep in mind that, at least at this point, this is just for your entertainment:

1. I naturally and easily say things like:
   A__ "I see what you mean"
   B__ "That sounds sensible to me"
   C__ "I have a good feeling for that"

2. When I encounter an old friend, I often say:
   A__ "It's great to see you again!"
   B__ "It's great to hear your voice again!"
   C__ "I've missed you!" (and give them a big hug)

3. I have:
   A__ a good eye for décor and color coordination
   B__ the ability to arrange the stereo and speakers so the music is crystal clear
   C__ a special feeling in my favorite rooms

4. I let other people know how I'm feeling by:
   A__ the clothes I dress in and the way I do my hair or makeup
   B__ the tone of my voice, sighs, and other sounds
   C__ my body posture

5. My favorite romantic encounters include:
   A__ watching the other person, or vivid visualization or fantasy
   B__ listening to the sounds the other person makes
   C__ touching and being touched by the other person

6. When I want to really, totally understand something:
   A__ I make pictures of it in my mind
   B__ I talk to myself about it
   C__ I roll it around until I have a good feeling for it

7. When deciding on an important action, I:
    A__ must see all aspects of the situation
    B__ must be able to justify the decision to myself and/or some-
    body else
    C__ know when it's the right decision because my gut feelings
    tell me so

8. When it's important to me to influence another person, I pay
    careful attention to:
    A__ the pictures I paint with my descriptions
    B__ the intonation and pace of my voice
    C__ what kind of emotional impact I can bring to the situation

9. When I'm bored, I'm more likely to:
    A__ change the way I look or how things around me are arranged
    B__ whistle, hum, or play by making sounds in my throat
    or chest
    C__ stretch, exercise, or take a hot bath

10. My favorite authors:
    A__ paint vivid pictures of interesting places
    B__ write dialogue that sounds true to life
    C__ give me a feeling for the story that is moving and meaningful

11. I can tell what another person is thinking by:
    A__ the look on their face
    B__ the tone of their voice
    C__ the vibes I get from them

12. When I'm reading a menu trying to decide what to order, I:
    A__ visualize the food
    B__ discuss with myself the various options
    C__ read the list and choose what feels best

13. I would rather:

A__ look at pictures in an art gallery

B__ listen to a symphony or rock concert

C__ participate in a sporting or athletic event

14. When I'm in a bar with a band playing, I find most interesting:

A__ watching the other people or the band

B__ closing my eyes and listening to the music

C__ dancing with or feeling close to the other people around me

15. A true statement is:

A__ "It's important how you look if you want to influence others"

B__ "People don't know a thing about you until they've heard what you have to say"

C__ "It takes time to really get in touch with another person's core self"

You can score it here:

___ A (Visual) ___ B (Auditory) ___ C (Kinesthetic)

Most people, when they take this test, will find that there is a definite preference for one system or another, but that preference is not more than five or ten points away from their least preferred system. A well-balanced person will have very similar scores for all three areas. A person with radically high or low scores in any one system may want to consider using some of the exercises in later chapters on building attentional flexibility to break up rigid old patterns of perception and broaden and enrich their viewing, hearing, and experiencing of life.

You may also find it interesting that your closest friends—the people you best understand—often score similarly to you on the test. Those you just can't figure out, no matter how hard you try, may score quite differently from you on the test. This doesn't mean that you should avoid people who have different modality preference systems; instead, it should give you an insight into (voice to? feeling for?) how you can have a wider range of friends and connections with others. For example, experiment with using language that matches those around you, and while doing so try to also experience the sensory realities that such language implies.

When we have this information about our children, it gives us a whole new range of tools for improving communication and understanding their style of learning. This helps us improve the way we communicate with them. It can also aid you in helping your child's teachers better understand how your child learns—and through that understanding change the way the child is taught.

This is an introduction to a new world of change. It shows, tells, and gives you a feeling for the possibilities that await you in the rest of the book. Before we get into the specifics of NLP and other change techniques, however, we must first engage in one of the most powerful of all NLP techniques: reframing, or learning to look at things in new and different ways. . . .

2

When Is a "Difference" a "Disease"?

A decadent civilization compromises with its disease,
cherishes the virus infecting it, loses its self-respect...

E. M. CIORAN (1911–1995), ROMANIAN-BORN FRENCH
PHILOSOPHER, *THE TEMPTATION TO EXIST,* 1956

THIS CHAPTER IS ABOUT what happens to children and adults—and to the larger human society—when individuals or groups are defined, categorized, and slotted. It's important that we understand this, in terms of its impact both on the individual and particularly on a society, because this is exactly what has happened in the recent past to those children and adults who are impulsive, distractible, restless, and risk takers—what has come to be known as ADD and ADHD. The framing that's currently wrapped around ADHD children is often destructive to self-esteem and demoralizing; by reframing their perspective, you give them hope and step into their world in a way that can be transformational.

Often labels are useful, and there are very good reasons that we use them, both as individuals and as a society. At other times, they can be insidious and destructive. As we heal ADHD—one person at a time—it is my belief that we're also healing our entire society or

11

our "ADHD-ogenic culture," to borrow a phrase from Dr. Edward Hallowell. So it's important that we first have an overview—a broad look at what labels are, how they come to be applied, and the impact they can have.

For example, I have a friend who, as he prefers to remain anonymous, I'll call Bill. This friend has a hereditary brain difference from normal people. He first learned about this when he was a very young child, and he now lives in retirement with his brain abnormality. There is no drug for his condition, and although numerous types of brain surgery and electroshock treatments have been tried on others over the years to correct his type of abnormality, none has ever worked. Many thousands of people were left dead or as mental vegetables as a result of such experiments over the past thirty centuries. If you were to perform a PET, SPECT, or MRI scan on Bill's brain, you would find that it is organized and wired differently from my brain or those of the vast majority of humanity. Odds are his brain is different from yours.

This difference is not only obvious on a medical scan; it's also obvious to anybody who spends ten minutes with Bill and observes his behavior.

Bill's brain abnormality was apparent to his teachers when he was a child. Recognizing his brain abnormality as something that would cause Bill problems in later life, his teachers did their best to try to get him to rewire his brain, or at least perform as if he didn't have this brain difference. "They really had my best interests at heart," he told me. "They knew that the whole world is set up for people like you and not for people like me. Even though it seemed to me at the time that they were brutalizing me and singling me out and ridiculing me for my difference, I know now that they were just trying to help me fit in and be a bit more normal. It was very painful as a child, however, to be identified as being so different just because I was left-handed."

Bill is lucky that he was born in the twentieth century. Five hundred years ago, if he'd allowed people to learn of his difference, the leaders of the Catholic Church (or any of several countries they controlled the governments of) could have declared him an apostate, heretic, demon, agent of Satan, devil, or witch, and he could have been put to death. At the very least, he may have been subject to torture or exorcism and ostracized from both the church and his profession. People of that era and earlier who shared Bill's brain abnormality often went to great lengths to hide from everybody but their parents the fact of their difference, and there are records of parents and physicians in medieval Europe who put young children to death when it was determined at a young age that they shared Bill's brain difference.

As it was, the worst thing that happened to Bill was that in the first few years of school, his teachers tied his left arm to his body so he couldn't use it. In later years, when he'd reach for things with his left hand, the nuns who were the teachers in the school he attended would painfully slap his hand with a ruler or shout across the room at him, startling and humiliating him enough to quickly switch to his right hand.

"Being left-handed is no longer a crime or a sign of demonic possession," Bill told me a few years ago. "It's not even any longer assumed that it means you're gay. Now it's just a major inconvenience. I suppose I should be grateful for that."

Grateful, indeed.

THE URGE TO CATEGORIZE

Our culture, from its earliest days seven thousand years ago in ancient Mesopotamia, has a history of wanting to put things into categories. Aristotle was a big fan of this: he came up with the notion that *everything* could eventually be broken down into some smallest atomic particle component and thus organized and labeled and put into a neat little box. Nicolaus Copernicus and René Descartes expanded on the idea, and the atomic theory of tiny particles and the universe-as-a-machine paradigms reigned supreme as the basic assumptions of science until about forty years ago. That was when physicists realized that many of these understandings were seriously flawed, and they were startled to discover that the universe and all the matter and energy in it are organized more like an idea or a living organism than like a clock or a machine.

Nonetheless, naming and classifying is appealing to people because it gives them a sense of understanding and control, even when the reality of the situation may not justify that. For example, just about everybody learned in school that electricity is the motion of electrons in a wire. But what about electricity that moves through space, such as radio waves, where there is no possible flow of electrons? Then electricity is a wave, we're told. But a wave of what and in what medium? Nobody knows. The fact is that nobody even knows what electricity is, in wires or in space. It's definitely *not* the flow of electrons, even through a wire, and experiments show that in space a single electron will behave like a wave in one circumstance and then like a particle in another. Oddly, experiments show that the most important variable that determines whether it's a particle or wave is if it's being observed by a human being. At this moment, scientists are confused about electricity, yet we talk about it as if we understand it, because we can manipulate some aspects of it. We create models of it, such as Ohm's Law, which work out most of the time, although they break down when pushed beyond the boundaries of normal temperatures and distances.

Remember a time when you were very proud of yourself for understanding something that at first seemed complex. Remember how good you felt? Smile and enjoy that feeling.

Our culture feels good about naming things: it gives us a sense of control. By identifying something, we've put it in a box, gotten a handle on it, and given it a clear focus, even if it's a totally made-up picture. Even though it's an abstraction, once it's named it assumes a sense of reality.

With ADHD, for example, there are dozens of different theories about its origin, what causes it, how the brain works or doesn't work to bring it about, and its meaning. In addition to the American Psychiatric Association's criteria, there are probably a hundred different "tests" being sold to help therapists or individuals determine if they "have" ADHD. And yet it's still an abstraction: a label that gives the veneer of reality to something that's there, certainly, but by no means neatly defined or completely understood.

This obsession with labeling and packaging abstractions into single words or acronyms is in many ways unique to Western civilization. Most other peoples don't engage in the practice of turning abstractions into nouns. Instead of saying "culture," for example, most Native American tribes use the phrase "people living together and interacting." Most societies, historically, have been far more precise in their use of language than our post-Aristotelian civilization.

Along with Aristotle's idea that all physical matter is classifiable came the idea that all humans are also classifiable. Everybody can be fit, one way or another, into some sort of a slot. Aristotle thought this "organization of humanity" was a splendid idea. He wrote several detailed pieces on how it rationalized slavery and how slaves should be kept and managed. After all, if there are different types of people, it must be that some are superior and some are inferior. Some are born to rule, and some are born to serve.

America's founding fathers believed this. It was easy to justify displacing and murdering the natives who'd lived in North America for ten thousand years: they weren't "fully human," but instead were, in the words of Benjamin Franklin, "mere savages." Thomas Jefferson knew it was appropriate to buy and own slaves to work his plantation and service his sexual needs. They were, in his eyes and for many of his contemporaries, only three-fifths human (and, to those same men, Native Americans were not at all human).*

The early 1800s saw Thomas Huxley and Charles Darwin propose theories that further codified the ownership of one human by another: life-forms (including humans) *evolve,* they wrote, and the fittest, most worthy, most capable of a species will inevitably conquer, dominate, or destroy the lesser, weaker, or more inadequate of the species. Huxley applied this to cultures and civilizations, while Darwin applied it most directly to biology, although both acknowledged the other's arena. (Huxley, Darwin's cousin, wrote first on the topic.) Abraham Lincoln believed the concept as well. While he technically "freed the slaves," he also wrote and said in speeches that Blacks were "a race apart" who should never be allowed to intermarry or share the workplace with the White representatives of what he believed to be the most highly evolved race.

The works of Huxley and Darwin were later used to justify the eugenics movement of racial or ethnic cleansing in the United States in the 1920s and 1930s, supported by highly visible people such as Henry Ford and Charles Lindbergh and leading to the forced sterilization of tens of thousands of "inferior" people of all races (mostly the "mentally inferior," selected by specially trained psychiatrists). When Hitler picked up the banner, his advertisements and posters printed in Germany showed American hospitals where forced sterilization was practiced and quoted American legislators and scientists in talking about the need to "cleanse the race of inferior elements."

---

*The percentage applied to Blacks by the U.S. government at the time in counting people to determine representation in Congress.

A dozen other European countries were practicing forced eugenics before Hitler came to power.

And on a chilling note, I recently heard a speech at an ADHD conference in California by a well-known geneticist who suggested that married couples with ADHD should refrain from having children, for fear of "further damaging our gene pool," and that one day our society may again have to consider exercising some control over who can have children and who cannot because of the proliferation of "genetic problems," including ADHD.

WHO'S IN CHARGE?

Our culture is set up along lines of hierarchy, and this is imprinted in our children from an early age. There are workers, managers, officers, directors, and owners; voters, town officials, state legislators, federal officials, and the president. There are state legislators, school board members, principals, assistant principals, teachers, assistant teachers, students, and parents. This organizational hierarchy runs from our largest to our smallest cultural units. We have social hierarchies, usually based on wealth or fame. Our religious institutions are hierarchical, reflecting the hierarchies we've developed socially. Families are hierarchical, with the pecking order traditionally descending from father to mother to oldest child through to youngest child (although younger boys outrank older girls in many cultures), a gender and age order that we again see reflected in our religions.

We love hierarchies and impose them on virtually every aspect of our lives and the world around us. We so completely assume that hierarchical social structures are normal that most people, when confronted with evidence of nonhierarchical social structures among many Native American tribes (for example), will simply disregard the evidence and assume something has been overlooked by anthropologists. It's not possible, our culture tells us, for there not to be some people at the top and some people at the bottom.

Implicit in any hierarchy are the notions of "what is good for the system" and "what is not good for the system." "Good" is rewarded; "not good" is punished or discouraged. And the system itself—through a relatively organic process, not any sort of weird conspiracy—determines what it will define as "good" and "not good."

In modern psychiatry and education, ADHD is currently considered "not good." This designation for rebellious and "non-normal" behaviors has a long history, but there have also been times when ADHD and other off-the-norm personality types were considered "good."

For example, when America first started, rebellion was considered good—at least rebellion against the British. Oddballs and eccentrics such as Ben Franklin (who almost certainly had ADHD, as his autobiography graphically reveals) and George Washington were valued and encouraged, and thinkers of the time such as Jefferson and Madison worked hard to constrain the powers of the new government.

Over time, though, that early government grew to the point where now about one in every three workers in America is being paid with state, local, or federal government funds. Roughly another third works for one of fewer than five hundred huge multinational corporations, which do business under tens of thousands of names. Of all the advertising on television and in nationally circulated magazines, for example, 75 percent is bought and paid for by only one hundred multinational corporations. These same one hundred companies now account for over 50 percent of all of the funding of public television. Large, monolithic, and hierarchical institutions have come to be "the system," and it is they who have defined for us what is "good" and "not good" or "useful" and "not useful" *for them*. "What's good for General Motors is good for America," said U.S. Secretary of Defense Charles Wilson in 1953. No national leader since then has disagreed and survived politically.

In this new world order of corporate and governmental omnipresence, desirable and undesirable norms of behavior have been redefined.

"Good" is conformity and compliance: doing what you're told, following your superiors' instructions carefully, and paying attention to what your superiors have decided is important. Children are taught this message from their first years of school.

"Not good" is nonconformity and noncompliance: asking questions, resisting authority, wandering off, or trying to do things your own way. In other words, "Don't behave like those ADHD people." Children also receive this message in school, often in discomfiting ways.

To those things that we as a society have decided are "good," we add an additional reward and label: we call them "normal." They're the way things should be, reflecting the standards and values of the social and cultural power structure of the time.

But what is "normal"?

There was a time in America when it was "normal" to kill other people. Bounties were paid for Indian ears or scalps by various governments and large-scale ranchers (a practice that continues to this day in parts of Brazil and other developing nations). Getting rid of the natives was good for *our* society, so killing was defined as *normal*. It was so normal, in fact, that it was held up as an ideal. I remember as a child playing "cowboys and Indians" with toy guns, acting out the winning-the-West story we'd seen on TV and in the movies. Everybody always wanted to be on the side of the cowboys, who we all knew were "the good guys" and would ultimately be the victors in the gun battle. In a few American subcultures today, killing is still considered good. Some gangs in Atlanta, Los Angeles, Detroit, and New York require a random murder as the price of admission to the club. And as a society, we've decided that it's best if we all get together and kill people who have broken our rules, so there are public killing chambers in more than half our states, as well as a national killing chamber at the federal prison in Leavenworth, Kansas.

On an individual basis, though, we've pretty much decided and agreed that killing is not a good thing. It's "not normal." Even killing with an automobile while drunk has, over the past two generations, been redefined from "unfortunate but normal" (in the 1950s, prosecutions were extremely rare) to criminal.

So in today's world, all behaviors, when we're evaluating them to determine if they should be called "normal," are viewed through the twin lenses of: first, "Is it good for the government or big corporations (which represent two-thirds of us)?" and second, "Is it good for everybody else (the remaining one-third of us)?" (Generally, the question of "Is it good for 'other-others,' such as wolves or insects or Native Americans?" doesn't even come into the equation.)

Can you remember a time when you were angry and it was justified? You felt good understanding that there was a purpose to your anger. Then you could release the anger and see more clearly. Understanding why labeling individuals as ADHD is done and why these labels are harmful may incite justifiable anger. Though the strategies in this book may not peel away the label that has been applied, they will help shift the perception that people with ADHD have of themselves and the perception that those who are part of their lives have of them. In so doing, we can better the lives of people with ADHD and those who are part of their lives.

THE "NORMAL" MACHINE

In *Mein Kampf* (My Struggle), Adolf Hitler defined three types of personalities among the general population that government had to concern itself with. The first type were the government's friends, the second could be largely ignored by government or marginalized as crackpots, and the third type had to be isolated, ostracized, or even marked for extermination. In my opinion, Hitler's third type was very probably his characterization of the ADHD individual.

Here's his summary of the first ("good" and "normal") group:

To it belongs all those whom independent thinking is neither inborn nor instilled by education, and who partly through inability and incompetence believe everything that is put before them in black and white [. . .]. They are not in a position, nor do they wish personally, to examine what is offered them. Their entire attitude towards all current problems can be led [. . .] almost exclusively by the outward influence of others.

The second (marginal) group are people

who, after long and bitter disappointments, have changed over to the contrary [view of the world] and no longer believe anything that is put before them [. . .]. These people are very difficult to handle, as they will always face the truth with mistrust.

The third group (which possibly would have included people with ADHD) Hitler felt represented the greatest threat to his new world order. They were those

whom natural gifts and/or education have taught to think independently, who try to form a judgment of their own about everything, and who submit most thoroughly everything to which they have been exposed to an examination and further development of their own.

Hitler knew he had to do something about these rebels and free-thinkers. During his reign, the use of mass-communication technology was perfected and strongly embraced by the Nazis, particularly propaganda minister Joseph Goebbels. They'd turned radio into an extraordinary tool for brainwashing, and this new mass-communication technology had even more promise than the ubiquitous radio. Hitler even believed it held the possibility of neutralizing this third group.

This new thought-control device was a machine that caused people to go into a virtually instant alpha/theta-wave state of mind, with their intellectual and discriminative abilities slowed down and their receptivity enhanced. When connected to this machine, your eyes cease their normal scanning motion for hours at a time, your respiration and heartbeat rate slow, and most people simply stop talking with others and withdraw into themselves and the machine. Like the rats who self-administer cocaine until they die, people hooked up to this machine will often spend such long periods of time attached to the machine that they sacrifice normal exercise and social activities, putting themselves at risk for obesity, heart disease, diabetes, and a host of other disorders.

Using this same machine, a method was developed to deliver messages directly into the now highly receptive brain. The ability to determine these messages was controlled by the government and, to raise funds for the war effort, sold to the largest of the corporations in Nazi Germany.

Hitler saw such great potential in this machine that he presented it to the world at the 1936 Olympics in Berlin, calling its first large-scale development and demonstration at the Olympics by the Germans proof of the superiority of Nazi technology. He privately exulted, "What good fortune for men in power that people do not think!" He looked forward to the day when the average German citizen would spend hours every day connected to his machine, their thinking skills suspended and their mind flooded with dozens of messages every hour that exhorted them to consume more and more of the products of Nazi-supported corporations and to unquestioningly support the Nazi government.

Of course, Hitler never saw that day. It wasn't until two decades after the 1936 Olympics, during the administration of Dwight D. Eisenhower and Richard Nixon, that America became the first country in the world where the average citizen spent more than an hour a day watching television. Today, that average exceeds 4 hours a day, and as a result historically normal social activities, such as joining a lodge, a sewing circle, or a bowling league—or enjoying the theater or the symphony or a book—have all but died. Sitting in front of a box that alters brain wave activity and brain chemistry for hours at a time, drinking in over twenty-five thousand carefully crafted, high-impact messages a year through both the TV and the internet is now what we call "normal."

It benefits the government and the hundred largest multinational corporations, which represent the majority of "us." *We* have decided that it is good and normal. People who choose to disconnect their TVs are lampooned as being uninformed, Luddites, cranks, or cultists: *they* are "abnormal." Their behavior doesn't work to the benefit of corporate or governmental America. ADHD-type characters are often shown on network television, but rarely in a positive light: they are the misfits, the malcontents, and the butts of jokes and sitcoms. Even the characters played by people like Robin Williams, while lovable, were never to be taken seriously. People who don't fit in and don't play the game are simply marginalized or discarded in TV programming, further encouraging all of us to do the same with those ADHD misfits we know.

If you shift your viewpoint, even for a minute, you'll see what a huge change has happened in America in the past seventy years. Even our political terms have been redefined for us by this media. *Conservative* has come to mean "in favor of policies that further the interests of big corporate, religious, and political institutions." *Liberal* has come to mean "in favor of policies that benefit or further the interests of the individual." In this context, most Democrats have become as "conservative" as most Republicans, and the Republicans of the pre-TV era would today be blasted as "liberals." This is a total change from the way the terms were used back in 1964, when I worked for Barry Goldwater's presidential campaign. Goldwater himself pointed out that "conservative" should mean "more freedom for the individual or local community," not government intruding into people's private affairs or siding with big corporate polluters against local people. When he began speaking out like this, he was quickly marginalized by network commentators (employees of one of those five hundred corporations), who focused mostly on his age and implicitly questioned his mental faculties.

This extraordinary shift in our definitions occurred at the same time that a shift in how we label behaviors happened, and the term ADHD has become a household phrase.

LIFE GOES ON

There's a perhaps apocryphal story commonly told among therapists about the famous psychotherapist Frieda Fromm-Reichmann. She had a client, a young woman, who came to her a bundle of nerves and fears. This young woman was certain that she would soon be the victim of a terrible disaster, that the government had been taken over by madmen, and that her life was in danger. She was socially paralyzed by her anxiety and afraid to leave her house. Fromm-

Reichmann spent three years with this woman helping her resolve her fears and adjust to the society in which she lived. Finally, she was pronounced cured and discharged from therapy. Two weeks later, this young Jewish woman was arrested by the Gestapo and sent to a death camp. Shortly thereafter, Fromm-Reichmann herself escaped Nazi Germany.

If we want our children or ourselves to succeed in this modern society, however we define success, we must largely live by its rules and adjust ourselves to its standards, even as those standards change from decade to decade. No matter how abnormal the rules of our world may seem when compared to the way our children's brains are wired, this corporate/government-dominated society now wields the economic, political, and police power to make itself the final arbiter of what is really "normal."

The important concept for people with ADHD to grasp, however, is that the concept of "normal" is not an absolute. It shifts like the sands of the desert, nearly always in ways that serve the institutions of power in a society. It has little to do with any theoretical or real ideal, little to do with what may best serve the human race as a whole, and generally little regard for the sensibilities of the "abnormal" individual.

Understanding this, you can turn things around for your child or yourself. People who have the collection of behaviors and ways of seeing the world that the psychiatric and pharmacological industries have termed ADHD can thus recover some shred of their self-esteem.

Children and adults with ADHD may not be "normal," but they can be vitally important.

It was that "abnormal" group, the one Hitler most feared and hated, that first resisted him. It was the "public school failure"* Winston Churchill who first led the forces that ultimately defeated

---

*A phrase Churchill's father used in a letter to describe his son.

Hitler. It was misfits such as Franklin and Washington who created our nation, and it was the second-grade dropout Thomas Edison who transformed the world in ways that were previously unimaginable with his inventions of the movie, the transcontinental teletype, and the electric light bulb.

BETTER DEFINITIONS

Perhaps a better way to look at *normal* and *abnormal* in the context of behavioral and thinking styles is: "Does this style of behaving and thinking help or hurt the person who has it, and how does it affect those around them?"

The ADHD adult or child who is merely a bit flighty may make significant creative contributions to their society and circle of friends. On the other hand, what we call ADHD can also lead a person to prison or life under a highway overpass. In an ideal situation, we'd just look at the behaviors or ways of thinking and ask the person, "Do you feel happy thinking and living this way?"

One of the pervasive myths of the psychological business is that *abnormal* is defined as "that which makes a person less happy and less functional or causes them to hurt those around them" and that *normal* is "that which makes a person happy and benefits those around them." But we cannot overlook the importance of social and cultural context. It's the air we breathe and the water we swim in through the course of our lives. It determines whether our behaviors are merely affecting us or affecting the larger society. And it's society's feedback that will ultimately determine whether a person—regardless of *normal* or *abnormal* labels—is happy and functional.

In my years of writing and speaking on the topic of ADHD, I've heard from many people that they or their ADHD children experience occasional depression or unhappiness, which they believe is the result of their ADHD. Often, they find a doctor who'll prescribe Prozac or some other antidepressant for them in an effort to push away the negative feelings that sometimes intrude on their lives.

There is no doubt that for chronically clinically depressed people, antidepressant medications appear to be a godsend. For other less extreme cases, though, these drugs may instead offer an unnatural and even dangerous disconnection from the experience of life itself, particularly for children who are still in the process of figuring out how to respond to adversity and the vicissitudes of life.

All adults and children have built-in mechanisms that tell them when things are right and when they're wrong. This human-animal mechanism dates back to our days as hunter-gatherers, warning us to notice that sound in the jungle or wonder what that smell ahead may be. When things don't work out, it's evolutionarily a good thing to learn from the experience, and one of the most effective ways we learn from experiences is to attach feelings to them. We attach fear and pain to the experience of kicking a porcupine or bear. We attach happiness and joy to playing with our family or accomplishing a job. We've learned this way since we first turned our head, moments after birth, and found a nipple, producing a flood of happy feelings as we were filled with warm, nourishing milk.

So if a person with ADHD occasionally doesn't have the success that they'd like, or encounters problems in their life that are the result of their ADHD, it's not necessarily a bad thing that they feel a bit depressed about it. More likely, it's an entirely healthy and reasonable response, a warning signal that should not be turned off or muted. It's a signal to change things, do something new or different, or learn new skills or new ways of doing things—but certainly not a body or mind's call for drugs.

WHERE THE WOUNDING OCCURS

Most people who grew up with ADHD and count themselves among the walking wounded will tell you that their wounds came not from the ADHD itself (unlike the tormented paranoid schizophrenic or the chronic depressive), but instead, like the left-handed person, from the response of the world around them to their ADHD. Only other people with ADHD understand them and the way they think and live their lives. Their disorganization or messiness or distractibility are seen by their boss or spouse or teachers as enemy behaviors—symptoms of moral or mental weakness or sloth. Their craving for new experiences and excitement is seen as an inability to make a commitment, a failure of will or emotional weakness, and unreliability in a world dependent on the predictable and reliable in order to work properly.

The wounding of most children with ADHD happens not from their ADHD itself and not from within, but from without. It's the world around them that inflicts its judgments and criticisms, just as it once did to left-handed people, and when those judgments include words like "bad," "lazy," "stupid," "crazy," "dysfunctional," "defective," or "disordered," then the wounding can cut very, very deeply.

In this regard, even labeling a person with "attention deficit disorder" is a form of wounding. It's an instant stigma. Few could imagine it being a pleasant experience to stand up among friends and peers and say, "I am the person here with a deficit," or "I'm the disordered one among this group."

Even if there hasn't been a formal diagnosis, the child with ADHD probably knows they are different from normal people. For many adults, this acknowledgment has been a darkly kept secret. As is true for many people who are visible in this field, I've had a large number of friends and relatives call me up after reading my books or books by another author to say, "I always thought I was the only one like this in the world. I always hid it as much as I could." And many choose to continue to hide it.

HEALING ADHD

The process of healing a person with ADHD involves at least three different areas of work.

First is the redefinition of the self, which is what the earlier parts of this chapter were designed to help you do for yourself and your children. By understanding how our concept of "normal" is derived and how it shifts with time, you can begin to reframe your perception of yourself and those around you.

While the traditional medical model has suggested this is necessary too, their redefinition involves the *disempowering* message that the person is the victim of a disorder, suffering from a deficit, implicitly not whole or functional, and that *only* the medical field holds the answers or "cure" for them.

An increasing number of people in the field, from psychiatrists to medical school professors to teachers to schoolchildren, are rejecting this definition. I reject it too. In my experience, giving a person this message is the moral and emotional equivalent of telling a rape victim that she "asked for it" by wearing provocative clothes. It blames the victim. It adds, literally, insult to injury.

Since my son was first diagnosed with ADHD and told by several different authority figures that he had a "brain disease," I have worked in my writing and speaking around the world to change this story. I do not deny that the constellation of behaviors we call ADHD exists, nor do I deny that it's a substantial problem, both for individuals with it and for the societal institutions that work with them. I do, however, reject the notion that it means illness and disease.

Each of my previous books has explained my conception of ADHD as a vestigial survival mechanism in considerable detail, so

I will treat it here in only short form: I believe that ADHD suits a person well to living in a hunting-gathering world, but that it puts them at a disadvantage in a farming or industrial world. Think of the skills the best hunters possess: they constantly monitor their environment; they throw themselves into the hunt and lose track of time; they react in an instant and change strategy just as quickly; they utilize incredible bursts of energy without noticing; and they leap into situations within a split second, without hesitation, and often without recognizing the danger that may exist.

Sound familiar?

For the first few hundred thousand years of human history, people with ADHD ruled the world as hunters, but now that over 98 percent of the world's population lives in an industrial or industrially developing world, ADHD has become a disadvantage . . . unless you're one of those who has learned how to reinvent your life to work with, instead of against, your neurological difference.

So step one is to redefine the self in relation to the rest of the world. It's not necessarily true that the world is right and functional and the self is broken and disordered. It may well be that the self is functional, and it's the society in which a person lives that is dysfunctional. Those who apply the ADHD label are often as confused about their lives as the ones being labeled. We see the angst of living detailed through the arc of history, from humankind's earliest writings to Freud's *Civilization and Its Discontents* to modern studies that show as many as a third of all Americans take mood-altering drugs. As I note at length in my book *The Last Hours of Ancient Sunlight,* we live in a world where forty-five thousand people die every day from starvation, over one hundred species go extinct every day, toxic and radioactive waste is sold as fertilizer and sprayed on crops, and children work in factories for ten dollars a week. Our society has brought us over twenty thousand nuclear weapons, an exploding population, and rapidly diminishing supplies of oil. Many people look at this situation and ask themselves, "Is this *really* the world that I'm being told to adapt to? Is this what they mean when they say 'normal'?"

While the pursuit of happiness, or Maslow's pursuit of self-actualization, are common and noble aims, most people only occasionally touch such places. This is the fate of those who live in modern society, and no credible researcher has ever demonstrated that it can be significantly changed by taking drugs or undergoing extensive psychotherapy. Life in this society is difficult, and all indicators suggest that the future will offer us more and more difficult challenges.

It is not a solution to apply a disempowering label to people. It's not even a solution to throw some drugs at them or toss them into "special" classrooms or give them workplace "accommodations."

Step one to the solution is for the child or adult to take back their own personal power, stand up straight, and say, "I am who I am, and that is OK for now." Acknowledging past failings and wounds is fine, so long as it's in the context of "And from here I will go forward."

Step one is to decide to begin where you or your child is and realize that your normal is every bit as valid as anybody else's normal, even if it's not the standard applied by the power structure that is polluting our planet to death. By reading this far and internalizing this message, you've now walked through step one: the reframing necessary to begin healing.

Step two is to learn specific skills. Learn how to reorganize the way your child conceptualizes time, for example, so they can learn to plan things for the future instead of waiting for a crisis. Learn how to excel quickly in a traditional classroom setting or the workplace and memorize easily. Learn how to not forget where things are. Learn how to motivate yourself. Learn how to find the courage to change your life, and help your child find the courage to change theirs. You will find each of these—and more—in this book.

Step three is to walk back through the past to all those times when ADHD caused pain or discomfort and recalibrate the memories, so they're available as learning experiences but no longer as sources of lingering pain. We'll deal with this, also, in the chapters that follow.

3

Life Is What We Think It Is

The basic tool for the manipulation of reality is the manipulation of words. If you can control the meaning of words, you can control the people who must use the words.

PHILIP K. DICK (1928–1982), AMERICAN
WRITER, FROM HIS 1978 SPEECH
"HOW TO BUILD A UNIVERSE THAT
DOESN'T FALL APART TWO DAYS LATER"

ONE OF MY BEST FRIENDS has lived in New York City his entire life. Jerry's had apartments in the SoHo or Chelsea districts of Manhattan and hasn't owned a car for years. He does volunteer work at a hostel uptown, goes to shows and restaurants regularly, and has an active life in the city, most of which involves walking or taking the subway from place to place. I've walked miles of New York with him over the past forty years, and never once have I seen him act afraid of "the jungle." Jerry's never been attacked or mugged, even though he drove a Manhattan taxi for a few years, and thinks of his city as a warm, friendly, interesting place. He can't imagine living anyplace else.

A few years ago, I visited Manhattan with a friend from the Midwest. Everywhere we went, my friend was constantly looking over his shoulder, worried that we were about to be attacked. He approached street corners and alleys with a wary eye and seemed to shrink when tough-looking kids on the street walked by us. He was utterly terrified. We spent a week in the city doing a trade show, walking around, and sightseeing, but he never got over his fear. At night, every siren or loud sound would wake him up, so during the day he was red-eyed and tired. He was never attacked, other than when a car honked at him as he crossed a street against the light, but to this day he talks about his "terrifying experience" of being forced to walk the streets of New York in order to do business that week.

Neither Jerry nor my other friend were ever attacked in New York City. Jerry, however, describes walking through the city as a relaxing way to spend an afternoon; my other friend would say it's a terrifying ordeal.

Who's right? Both of them.

Reality, to a very large extent, is what we make it with our minds.

While it may appear that we live in a "real" world, we actually live much of our lives in a world made of our own thoughts, ideas, and feelings. Every bit of sensory information, in order to become meaningful, must first pass through the filter of our worldview, our meaning-attributing mechanism. "Primitive people," when seeing a tree sway in the wind, see the hand of a god. "Scientific people," observing the same thing, see the action of gaseous molecules in motion—wind—on the surface area of the leaves. For each, their observation is a clear and definite "reality."

REDEFINING REALITY

When we understand how much influence our beliefs and assumptions have on how we perceive and experience the world, we can then begin the process of changing the beliefs and assumptions that are not useful to us.

A good starting point for this redefinition process is in the notion of self-identity—where a person fits into the overall larger scheme of social and cultural life.

For example, consider what would happen if you were to dump the label of *diseased, disordered,* or *defective.* How would your life be different if, instead, you started looking at your own or your child's ADHD as "Hunter qualities" and searched out those particular "Hunter skills" that are the most useful? Using this model of reality, you would now have the power to identify the behaviors and strategies you have that you'd like to keep, those you'd like to get control of, and those you'd like to get rid of.

Beliefs are concepts or ideas to which we have attached a sense of reality, whether it's warranted or not. Most beliefs are quite useful. While you don't *know* that tomorrow morning the sun will come up, you have a lifetime of experience indicating it will, so it's a pretty reasonable, and even useful, belief to have. (People who don't share this belief tend to have rather miserable lives, going through their days with an unreasonable fear that the sun won't rise again.)

Other beliefs we're less certain about. Will the car start in the morning? Will I still have a job tomorrow? Will the stock market crash? Will I remain in my current state of health or sickness? We certainly have opinions and hopes. But to classify these as beliefs, we'd have to add the adjective *weak* before the word *beliefs.*

And there are the *very* weak beliefs—the ones that we're more wishful about than anything else. One of these lottery tickets may be a winner. Maybe that person across the room will ask me to dance. Perhaps if I mail in this Publishers Clearing House Sweepstakes form, I'll win a million dollars.

Regardless of their strength, another way to characterize beliefs is to say that beliefs are stories we tell ourselves about how things are.

In addition to categorizing beliefs as being strong or weak, we can also define beliefs as those that are useful and those that are not useful. This is a pragmatic approach, and one that must be done with careful deliberation, as our beliefs echo through all other aspects of our lives. When we confront and analyze our beliefs, we can determine which ones are keeping us from success and happiness and which are keeping us from even trying to succeed or be happy. If you have or know someone with ADHD, you may find the beliefs you hold about yourself or the person you know are not even your own but have been created by society.

IDENTIFYING AND CHANGING LIMITING BELIEFS

Limiting beliefs are those stories we tell ourselves that cause us to sabotage our own best efforts. They hurt and cripple our lives, diminish our abilities, or hold us back from reaching our goals. Everyone has limiting beliefs. Everyone can change them. Most people don't realize it's possible to change them and, for that matter, don't even realize that they ever made a decision in their lives about what to believe and what not to believe.

For example, I recently had lunch with a fellow who was a brilliant guitarist. Ralph had played coffeehouses for years and then quit playing when he was offered a recording contract by a record label.

"Why'd you quit music?" I asked him.

"It lost its sparkle," he said, "when they started offering me money to do it. I realized that I was getting too good, too commercial. From there to selling your soul to the music industry is just one small step, so I decided to stop moving in that direction."

This is an example of a limiting belief. As with most, it contains a kernel of truth—some people do sell out their art and are miserable as a result of it, or they may be very happy but have done their art form damage through exploiting it commercially. But most people who are successful as artists don't have this limiting belief, and most are able to continue producing "good art" even when they become commercially successful. (Some, like John Lennon or Pablo Picasso, even seem to become *more* brilliant as artists when they achieve commercial success.)

Probing a bit deeper, it turned out that Ralph had multiple limiting beliefs. A second one was that "all people who are financially successful are jerks, because to be financially successful you have to sell out to the establishment." Again, there are cases where this is true, but it doesn't have to be so.

These two beliefs combined synergistically in Ralph. He'd developed them when he was a frustrated and mostly unemployed musician as a way of keeping his own self-esteem intact. *He* hadn't sold out to the establishment; *he* hadn't compromised his art for money. It was a way of being part of an aristocracy, a type of reverse snobbery. Whenever he saw a famous musician being fawned over by fans or going to an awards ceremony in a limousine or being paid millions for a new album, it confirmed to him what a sellout they were. Whenever he worked for nothing or played on street corners with his guitar case open and made five dollars an hour, it confirmed to him that he was not a sellout.

This set of beliefs served Ralph well for years. They kept him playing and practicing and improving his music, even though he had to work as a taxi driver and as an orderly in a hospital to put food on the table. It was all the necessary sacrifice to create truly good art, he told himself.

Then somebody offered him money for his music, and a chance to be "successful." This new reality collided head-on with his old beliefs, and he was unable to take advantage of the opportunity that, in many ways, he'd been working toward his entire life.

CHOOSING BELIEFS

At this point in his life, Ralph was paralyzed. He stopped playing his music altogether, because it reminded him of the conflict he'd run into. It was "no longer fun."

I asked Ralph if he'd like to be playing music again.

"That's a strange question," he said. "If I wanted to, wouldn't I be doing it?"

His response reminded me of a story I heard years ago, attributed to the famous hypnotist and psychiatrist Milton Erickson. In the version I heard of this possibly apocryphal story, a man came to Erickson and said, "I know I should eat spinach for my health, but I hate the stuff. Can you hypnotize me so I'll eat it?"

"Sure," said Erickson.

"Can you hypnotize me so I'll eat it once a week?"

"No problem," said Erickson.

"Can you hypnotize me so I'll eat spinach every day?" the fellow asked.

"Of course," said Erickson. "That's easy."

The fellow thought for a moment, then said, "Aw, forget it."

"Why?" asked Erickson.

The man replied, "Because I hate spinach."

The problem is that the limiting belief is so strong and so vivid and so out in front of everything else that the person can't even imagine other possibilities.

So the first step is to help a person imagine some other, different, new way of living that doesn't involve the limiting belief. It requires them envisioning how life would be if they left it behind or were able to change it.

I asked Ralph if he knew of any musicians who'd sold out their art for money. Of course, he had a substantial list of people who'd become famous and then begun to turn out cookie-cutter plastic music. I expected he'd have such a list, since accumulating it over the course of his life would have served to keep intact his old beliefs in the moral superiority of not making money from music.

Then I asked him if he knew of anybody who'd kept their artistic integrity after they began to make money. He emphatically said, "No." His belief not only had self-reinforcing mechanisms built into it, but it also had blinders on either side of it so it wouldn't see anything that contradicted it. I'd have to go in through a side door.

"How'd you first get interested in music?" I asked.

"I was a kid," he said. "It was the sixties, and the Beatles were hot, and I wanted to be a rock star. Then I got into listening to people like Dave Van Ronk and John Fahey and Tom Rush and decided I wanted to do folk music. I guess I ended up doing some of both. Most of the songs I've written are a bit of both."

"Like James Taylor?" I said.

"In some ways, I suppose," he said. "Really, my style is my own. I don't imitate anybody else."

"Isn't that true of most successful musicians?"

"No," he said emphatically. "Pat Boone and Elvis Presley were hired by the record companies specifically to do the music that was then being very successfully performed by Black artists. But the record companies didn't want to hire Black artists, so they got guys like Boone and Presley to do that same music. Neither of them was at all original."

"What about Frank Zappa?" I asked.

Ralph smiled. "Zappa was original. No doubt about it. Particularly his early stuff with The Mothers of Invention."

"The Beatles?"

"They started out doing what everybody else was doing, the same old clunk, clunk, clunk music. But with their *Sgt. Pepper's* album, and *The White Album,* they really began to get into some creative stuff."

"Wasn't that after they became successful?" I asked.

He frowned. "Yeah, I guess it was."

"So at least one group was able to keep its artistic integrity through fame, right? And even grow it?"

"Yeah, I guess so."

"There have to be others," I said.

His eyes searched the ceiling for a moment, then he said, "I guess you could say that about Frank Zappa too. Look at his later work, his symphonic stuff. The guy was a genius."

"Woody Guthrie?"

"Yeah, for sure. And Pete Seeger. He used his fame to deliver his message. Like 'Little Boxes.'"

At that point, I'd put a crack in his limiting belief. Other people had, it turned out, been successful and not ended up artistically dead because of it. Now to turn the light coming through that crack onto Ralph.

"So, Ralph, what was the difference? What made John Lennon and Frank Zappa stay true to their art, and even get better at it, whereas others turned into cookie-cutter music factories?"

He looked down at his legs for a moment, then said, "I guess they had a stronger commitment to their music. For them, the music was more important than the money."

Here was a new possible belief for Ralph. It may or may not be "true," but it could certainly be useful, so I thought I'd give a try at installing it. (Keep in mind that he came to me in the first place because he wanted to be playing his music again.)

"Ralph, are you more strongly committed to music or to money?"

He looked startled, then sat up straight. "I'm more committed to music than to money! That's why I gave up the music: they started offering me money for it!"

"Can you imagine a picture of what your life would be like if you had a lot of money *and* you had the time and a place to make good music?"

He looked right at me. "I don't think . . ."

"Look up to the ceiling, Ralph, and ask yourself if you can imagine what you would look like in a situation like that."

He looked up and seemed to be searching around for a moment, then smiled. "Yeah, I can see myself living a comfortable life and also making music."

"You're strong enough to take the money and still make music that is pure and true to your art?"

"Hell yes!"

"Could you have money and not become a jerk?"

He glanced back up at the ceiling, where he'd made his mental image, and checked it out. "Yeah, sure. I can do that."

"I wonder what the air would smell like in that time and place you're imagining yourself? I wonder what the sounds would be?"

He looked up for a moment, then down, then said, "There would be music all the time. My music. And the air would smell fresh like a forest because I'd build a big house out in the forest, with a recording studio in the barn."

"Now, can you think of anything else that would hold you back?" I asked.

He looked down for a moment and said softly, "I have ADD. Just discovered it last year, but it's obviously been there my whole life. And so I probably couldn't be successful because of the disorder."

Here was another limiting belief that Ralph was holding that kept him from even trying to succeed. I needed to crack it, too, although I knew I couldn't convince him that the ADD didn't exist, that he didn't have it, or that it wasn't a problem: we both shared beliefs in the "reality" of ADD (even though our meanings of that reality were radically different). So there had to be another way.

"Do you think any of the successful musicians you've known or known of in your life have had ADD?" I said.

He looked up for a moment, then said abruptly, "Zappa, for sure. He was a madman. You ever see him on TV being interviewed?"

Whether Frank Zappa had ADD or not was irrelevant at that moment if Ralph could *believe* Zappa did, and then use that belief to complete his own internal role model. "I haven't seen him interviewed, but he sure did hop around a lot, musically," I said. "Wouldn't surprise me if he was easily bored at least."

"At *least*," Ralph said. "And John Lennon. Look at all the wild stuff he did, compared to, for example, Paul McCartney, who's been so steady and straight-ahead. I'll bet Lennon had ADD too."

"So it's possible for a person with ADD to be a successful musician?"

"Yeah!"

"Can you still see that picture of yourself making music successfully, even with your ADD?"

He looked up for a few minutes, took a deep breath, and then said, "Yep. Absolutely."

MODELING OTHER PEOPLE'S BELIEFS

In talking with Ralph, what I had him do was find for himself an internal role model. Even though he'd never met John Lennon or Frank Zappa, he could still use them as internal role models. He could make up stories about their motivations and behaviors and life's problems, and then use those stories as models for himself about how he could be.

"But that's making things up!" one person remarked to me in a seminar I was teaching on this material.

"Of course it is!" I said back in the same tone of voice. As humans, we lack the ability to pop into another person's head and read their thoughts, desires, and motivations. All we can do is make observations of them and their behaviors, and then form conclusions based on those observations. It's all made up in our own heads anyway—none of us can truly read other people's minds!

One very effective way to change limiting beliefs is to find another person who has the same "problem" but who apparently doesn't share that limiting belief—a person who has figured out some other, more useful belief and is living it in their life. Particularly useful in the context of ADHD are historical figures who sure look like they must have had ADHD—like Winston Churchill, John Kennedy, or Ben Franklin—and read their biographies to learn how they overcame their ADHD symptoms (Franklin's autobiography is particularly useful for this). Visualize that person living their life with their empowering belief. Then visualize yourself in that same situation. Check out how you feel about it. If it feels OK, then step into yourself in that visualization and experience the reality of the new belief. Ask yourself what it will sound and smell and feel like as a way of moving right into the experience.

PRESUPPOSING CHANGE IN BELIEFS AND BEHAVIORS

One of the most effective ways to facilitate and ensure change is to convince people that the change is inevitable. Doing this consciously, however, is often somewhere between difficult and impossible. It's much easier to speak to the unconscious.

For example, a child was brought to see me who, at the age of eight, was still dragging around his childhood blanket and sucking his thumb. He'd been hassled considerably about it, mostly by his older sister and his well-intentioned grandparents, who lived nearby. As a result, he'd developed a lot of anxiety around the issue and, it came out, actually believed that he may be dragging the blanket around for the rest of his life. That thought, as much as any other, haunted him.

Instead of challenging his reality at a conscious level, I posed a question which *presupposed* the change as already being in the process of happening. In the course of a friendly conversation about people we've all known who've had childhood habits that eventually went away, I said, "I wonder how many weeks it'll be before you feel good knowing that your blanket is back in your bedroom while you're somewhere else?"

He nodded, as if he were slightly confused but wanted to agree, and then I changed the subject back to talking about his friends and other things. But that one sentence was what the entire session was all about. It delivered to his *unconscious* mind several direct statements of an "already a done-deal fact": (1) a time would come when he'd no longer need to drag around his blanket, (2) it would actually feel good, and (3) it would happen within a period of weeks. Within three or four minutes of my having made that statement, I (and his mother, who was sitting in on the session) noticed a rather dramatic change in his body posture and tone of voice when he discussed his blanket. Before the statement, he'd pull his knees up to his chin and hold the blanket to him; after it, he simply sat with it on the chair beside him in his right hand. The change had already begun to work.

Such interventions are classic examples of the work of Erickson, Bandler, and Grinder, among others. The "I wonder when . . ." statement is a powerful way to influence people, particularly children, without directly challenging their limiting beliefs. It goes around the beliefs, to the back door of the mind as it were, and delivers to the unconscious mind an opportunity to experience the possibility of a new reality.

In another similar case, a child who'd been diagnosed with ADHD, largely because of his dislike of homework, heard, "I wonder how long it'll be before you discover the secret to making homework fun that so many of the A-grade students know?" Notice the presuppositions in there. The child then began a hunt to "discover the secret" and eventually found it! (Of course, it was merely a technique, one of the strategies in my book *ADD Success Stories* of breaking homework into short sessions and doing them throughout the evening.)

Whether you're dealing directly with an ADHD behavior (which is a very loose and slippery definition) or a specific behavior that may arise from, have to do with, or impinge on the life of a child with ADHD, this technique can be very useful.

I wonder how many hours it'll be before you try it out with your child in a way that's helpful, supportive, and healing?

4

What Is ADHD?

He who considers disease results to be the disease itself,
and expects to do away with these as diseases, is insane.
It is an insanity in medicine, an insanity that has
grown out of the milder forms of mental disorder in
science, crazy whims.

JAMES TYLER KENT (1849–1916), AMERICAN
HOMEOPATHIC PHYSICIAN, *THE ART AND*
SCIENCE OF HOMEOPATHIC MEDICINE, 1900

NOBODY KNOWS WHAT attention deficit hyperactivity disorder (ADHD) is, exactly; why it is; or where it comes from. There are, however, a variety of theories that are commonly presented in books, doctors' offices, and at conferences. They include:

1. *ADHD is a brain disease or an indication of brain damage.*
   This is the most extreme of the medical models, espoused mostly by people selling "cures" and "therapies" that range from radiation injections for brain scans to blue-green algae to a variety of psychoactive drugs. This model assumes that something is wrong: somehow the brain has become twisted or distorted or damaged and is not functioning properly. Because this model is rooted in the "body as a machine" view of medicine, the search

is for the "defective part" and the way to fix it. Parts that have
been pointed to include deficiencies or excesses of various neurotransmitters (dopamine, serotonin, the adrenaline substances,
acetylcholine, and others), brain structures (damaged or underdeveloped frontal lobes, occipital lobes, parietal lobes), and general nervous system dysfunctions (chiropractic subluxations).

2. *ADHD is a physiological reaction to the environment.* This
theory was first championed by Dr. Benjamin Feingold when he
discovered that some of his pediatric allergy patients experienced
behavior improvements when they were put on an allergen-free
diet to control skin disorders such as psoriasis. Other environmen-
tal culprits that have been championed by various people include
lead, milk allergies, wheat allergies, sugar, pesticides, salicylates,
TV, general poor nutrition, sunlight deprivation, and a lack
of exercise.

3. *ADHD is a psychological reaction to the environment.* This
theory has been around the longest. For hundreds of years, parents of ADHD children (even before the diagnostic category was
invented) have been accused of poor parenting. Other variations
on this include ADHD being caused by physical, sexual, or emotional abuse; children with above- or below-average IQs not fitting into a standardized classroom environment; children getting
in with the "wrong crowd" and not valuing school or the opinions of teachers or parents; a psychological meltdown response
to collapsing and imploding social structures; developmental lags
while growing up; and growing up in deprived environments.

4. *ADHD is a normal and natural part of the spectrum of
human behavior but not as useful in modern society as it may
have been in the past.* This theory is my personal favorite, and I
believe it to be true, but it has no more or less proof arguing for it
than any of the others. It's detailed quite thoroughly in my book
ADHD: A Hunter in a Farmer's World.

I'd noticed early on that the cardinal characteristics of ADHD—distractibility, impulsivity, and a love of novelty/sensation/risk—were all things that would be adaptive in a society where food was acquired by hunting and gathering. The "distractible" hunter would constantly be scanning the forest looking for food and watching out for dangers and predators. While that scanning behavior is maladaptive in a classroom, it would become necessary for survival in a primitive environment. Similarly, impulsivity—the ability to make an instant decision and be acting on it before the thought process has even caught up—would be necessary in a world where only the nimble could instantly respond to changes (the sighting of prey or predator). A thoughtful risk/benefit analysis approach to decision-making in such an environment would doom one to death; the "impulsive" tendency to make quick decisions on an almost unconscious level would be necessary. Similarly, the love of risk and new sensation associated with ADHD would be useful in a world full of risks, but it would lose its usefulness when the transition was made to the relatively safe and sedentary world of living on the farm.

Suffice it to say that I'm convinced (as are many anthropologists, psychologists, psychotherapists, and psychiatrists) that in a hunting/gathering society, the same characteristics that make ADHD a liability in modern society would make it an asset—indeed, a survival mechanism—in humankind's historic natural environment. Additionally, when we look at members of the few remnant societies of this sort still left on Earth, we find extremely high levels of what could be called ADHD-like behaviors, and it is these same behaviors of constantly scanning the environment (distractibility), quickly making decisions and acting on them (impulsivity), and loving new and novel activities (risk taking) that help them survive.

5. *ADHD is a myth made up by greedy drug companies and doc-tors eager to increase their income, or incompetent teachers looking to place the blame for children's academic failures away from themselves.* This theory is the favorite of Rush Limbaugh and his ilk, has appeared in the *Wall Street Journal,* and is the sub-ject of several books. Based on the kernel of truth that there is no identifiable physiological marker or blood test available to defini-tively identify a person with ADHD, it's been virtually turned into religious dogma by those who view the medical and educa-tional professions with disdain. It's championed by the Church of Scientology. It's the subject of an otherwise thought-provoking book, *The Myth of the ADD Child* by Thomas Armstrong. And it's particularly attractive to those who have become radicalized by encountering the "shoot 'em up with radiation" doctors or the "it's all just bad parenting or child abuse" advocates.

THEY'RE ALL JUST GUESSES

As of 1997, when the first edition of this book was written, none of the above theories had been proven to be the one-and-only cause of ADHD behaviors or ADHD labeling, and it's the opinion of some in the field that time will eventually show it to be a collection of the above factors. As of this 2020 edition, it's now clear that there's a huge genetic component to ADHD (documented in more detail in my book *ADHD: A Hunter in a Farmer's World*), but genes also interact with the environment, both physical and psychological.

At its core, ADD is generally acknowledged to be made up of the three primary behaviors of *distractibility, impulsivity,* and *risk taking.* If you throw in the inability to sit still, or *hyperactivity,* you have ADHD. The symptoms are essentially the same between children and adults, and between men and women, although there are some differences in the emphasis of symptoms that are unique to each group. These three characteristics show up in a variety of ways, rang-ing from general disorganization to procrastination to difficulties in school or relationships, and these secondary results of the behaviors are the most common focus of attention when working with people who have ADHD.

Numerous questionnaires and tests are available to score a per-son's level of ADHD (it's not all or nothing, but a spectrum of severity), which range from the free test published in the American Psychiatric Association's *Diagnostic and Statistical Manual* (*DSM*) to ones for which the publishers or test administrators charge as much as a hundred dollars for a dozen printed sheets of paper. Only the *DSM* questionnaire is "official" in the United States, although that hasn't stopped any number of medical entrepreneurs from hoping to cash in on the ADHD craze in the same way Meyers and Briggs became wealthy from the fad of psychologically typ-ing people and using that information in business. All of these questionnaires use a variety of questions to determine historically how a person has behaved in the three or four areas mentioned above, although a few of the private tests stretch the definitions of ADHD beyond the American Psychological Association's (APA) realm.

For adults, probably the best test is published in the book *Driven to Distraction* by Edward Hallowell, MD, and John J. Ratey, MD. For diagnosing children, the *DSM* criteria are quite ample, and the APA's *DSM* book is available in most large bookstores or libraries. Nearly all these tests carry the caveats that the symptoms must have been present lifelong, they must not be the result of some other identifi-able mental or physical illness, and the symptoms—which nearly all people, having ADHD or not, share in some small measure—must be frequent and severe enough to represent a significant step away from the norm.

DISINHIBITION OR DIFFERENT BASELINES?

One of the most popular theories about ADHD posits that it's a function of underdeveloped or genetically ill-formed frontal lobes of the brain, that part just behind the forehead. The frontal lobes are the portions of the brain where, it is believed, time is sensed. If this is where time is sensed, so the theory goes, then this is also where a person may plan and organize, learning from the past and projecting that learning into the future. This could make the frontal lobes the seat of the abilities to inhibit behavior, wait on a short-term reward in order to later get a better long-term reward, and postpone pleasure. Ignoring the fact that humans are the only animals with well-developed frontal lobes and yet other animals have been trained to postpone gratification, these theorists assert that ADHD is a disorder of distractibility, impulsivity, and risk taking so much as it is a lack of inhibition. If a person were properly inhibited, they say, then they wouldn't have problems with distractibility, impulsivity, and risk taking.

It's a nice theory, but it suffers from a fundamental underlying flaw in the opinion of some critics. It fails to address the issue of baseline states of desire or motivation toward these behaviors.

If you were to take two equally inhibition-capable people who had recently had lunch and walk down the street with them, telling them both to not look into the windows of restaurants and food shops, you probably would find that both were capable of performing that exercise with little or no effort. Both could contain their impulses and curiosity for the benefit of the experiment. However, if you were to prevent one of those people from eating for two days, the result would probably be quite different. And if you'd starved one of the people for a week or more, you may not even be able to prevent that person from *entering* the store and ordering some food!

While the advocates of the "inhibition-failure theory" are proposing that the biggest problem for people with ADHD is learning how to inhibit their behaviors, if you ask people with ADHD about this theory, you'll often hear a somewhat contradictory response. They frequently describe a lifetime of feeling drawn, nearly compulsively, to new stimulation, new sensations, and new experiences, like a hungry man is drawn to a meal. Most are quite competent at inhibiting themselves in many parts of their lives and have been successful in those particular realms. But when one of their craving buttons is hit, the level of internal pressure can be so intense it overwhelms otherwise normal inhibitory mechanisms.

In my book *ADHD: A Hunter in a Farmer's World,* in a chapter titled "What Maslow Overlooked," I proposed a detailed hypothesis to explain the mechanism driving this process, combining known neurology (thalamic function) and classic humanistic psychology. I continue to believe that this is the mechanism that underlies ADHD—a drive and a hunger to fulfill the basic human need to experience *aliveness.* This need is so visceral that people will violate the needs for safety, approval, and even relationships to get it met.

Over the past few years, a number of studies have been done in Israel and the United States on what is called "novelty-seeking behavior." An inherited gene has been identified that's associated with this behavior, and it's theorized that this gene causes brain levels of at least one neurotransmitter—probably dopamine—to be slightly different in these people than in people without the gene configuration.

I've been watching these studies with great interest, wondering if perhaps what these researchers are studying is the mechanism that underlies much of what we call ADHD. If the novelty-seeking urge is strong enough, it'll overwhelm any learned inhibition, regardless of how well intentioned the person may be. The people who were found with this gene in the initial studies also reported having what many in this country would call "ADHD lives": they are racecar drivers, parachutists, and entrepreneurs and have the whole range of high-risk, high-stim life patterns. They also showed a greater tendency to have failed marriages, multiple jobs, and even multiple careers; to have had difficulty in school; and to make impulsive decisions. Time will tell, of course, how this all shakes out. For the moment, there are those who would be dismayed if ADHD turned out to be "simply" an overabundance of novelty-seeking behavior. It could threaten a billion-dollar industry (treating and medicating ADHD), while calling into question many of our assumptions about what is "normal."

In the meantime, people growing up with diagnosed or undiagnosed ADHD in modern societies are likely to experience humiliation, frustration, and an intense struggle with the ordinary events of school and life to a degree that is often unimaginable to those not touched by the condition.

5

How People Are Damaged by Growing Up with ADHD

I am convinced that, except in a few extraordinary cases, one form or another of an unhappy childhood is essential to the formation of exceptional gifts.

THORNTON WILDER (1897–1975), AMERICAN WRITER, INTERVIEW IN *WRITERS AT WORK*, 1958

TELL THEM THEY'RE BAD AND THEY BECOME BAD

One of the first rules of child-rearing is "condemn the behavior, not the child." Numerous studies over the past century have confirmed the common sense notion that what you repeatedly tell children about themselves is what they will come to believe. It'll become the staging ground for the rest of their lives. "Train up a child in the way he should go: and when he is old, he will not depart from it," says the author of Proverbs 22:6, and no competent psychologist or psychiatrist today would argue with the wisdom of that sentiment.

This being the case—and there are few who would dispute it—consider the impact on a young child being told that they have a brain disease, and further being told that this disease often causes people with it to become school dropouts, criminals, and failures in life. The name of this disease identifies quite specifically how the brain works: it is deficient and disordered. The child cannot pay attention.

Never mind the fact that the child can sit in front of the television for hours without moving, can beat all their friends at video games, and has become a hero of the skateboard crowd; they have a disorder of the brain and are . . . well . . . defective. Damaged goods. Born that way. Nothing to do about it except take a pill, and that's not a cure, just a way of controlling their out-of-control brain for a few hours at a time.

"Attention deficit hyperactive disorder" is one of the clearest medical articulations I've encountered of the "born to lose" label that rebellious teenagers applied to themselves in the 1950s, following the traditions of James Dean and Marlon Brando. You're doomed, kid. "Don't even bother with worrying about getting into college," my son was told by a psychologist. "ADHD kids just don't do well academically." Hundreds of parents have related similar stories to me over the years.

While this labeling may not be the first wounding that ADHD children and adults experience in life, it is often one of the most severe, particularly for kids. Adults, more often than not, seem to accept an ADHD label as a form of liberation: "At *last* I know what's been going on with me all these years!" they'll say. But for children, it's usually quite different. The childhood social imperative is to fit in, to be one of the crowd, to not be different at any cost. But when your brain is "diseased," how can you avoid being different? Many a teenager has related to me the pain and humiliation they experienced years earlier, when first made to wear the ADHD label for teachers and peers to see.

The obvious solution to this is to help children redefine for themselves the meaning of having ADHD. With things like the Hunter/Farmer model, we can provide a positive paradigm for self-image that still acknowledges the challenges a child or adult with ADHD will face in this postindustrial world.

SELF-ESTEEM AS A PREDICTOR OF FUTURE SUCCESS

In his best-selling book, *Emotional Intelligence*, Daniel Goleman lays out in great detail how the factors that contribute to a happy, well-adjusted adulthood are not necessarily good grades or even a high IQ. In fact, study after study has shown that there's virtually no correlation between grades in school and success in adult life.

Grades are not only an artificial indicator of a person's abilities, they're a recent invention. Thomas Jefferson, who was both President of the United States and founder of the University of Virginia, was completely unfamiliar with the concept. They didn't have grades when he went to school. People either succeeded or they didn't, and the fact of success or failure was a decision arrived at jointly between the teacher and the student.

The idea of grading students was first proposed by William Farish, a tutor at Cambridge University in England. It simplified his workload: he didn't have to get to know students firsthand, didn't have to have any insight into their depth of understanding or their ability to relate disparate concepts, and didn't have to help them struggle with the last 5 percent of understanding to completely get their minds around a concept. If he could simply measure their ability to memorize, he thought, he had an easy-to-use tool for determining their worth as a student and their probable success upon graduation.

Unfortunately for Farish, his students, and generations of students since his 1792 invention, grades do *not* predict success and, in fact, are not even a particularly good measurement of true learning or understanding of a topic. Studies of valedictorians have found that they're about as likely as anybody else to succeed or fail in life. Oddly enough, it's the "average students" who seem the most well-adjusted to life as adults—assuming, of course, that they were not constantly harassed, humiliated, or prodded by their parents or teachers to improve their grade point averages (GPA). Those adults who lived under the most pressure as students—and often got the best grades—are also often the ones who crumble under the pressures of life as adults.

Along with grades came another horror for students, although it's only been in the past few decades that it's become an obsession in the public schools: standardized curriculum. If grading students frees teachers from having to get to know them, work one-on-one with them, and develop any deep sense of their skill levels, then standardized curriculum causes them to not even have to think about what level of development or knowledge a student may be at. All students must be the same! It's ordained by the all-knowing bureaucrats in their offices downtown, in the state capitol, and in Washington, D.C.

Since the standardized curriculum has implicit in it a concept of normalcy, if students are not performing well, it's obviously through no fault of their teachers or their schools, but because *they* are not normal.

Unfortunately for our children, standardized curriculum has proven to be as much of a failure in helping kids learn as having grades. The ability to perform to some mythic norm is irrelevant as a measurement of a child's abilities, just as grades are only marginally relevant as a measurement of anything other than a person's ability to memorize information and take a test. (Neither of those skills have much application in the real world, and yet they make up the vast majority of what students are called upon to do throughout their school careers.)

There is, however, one measurable index that does a pretty good job of measuring a child's probability of leading a happy and successful life as an adult: self-esteem.

Self-esteem, however, is not generally measured in schools. Indeed, at times it seems as if modern schools were set up specifically to minimize self-esteem, producing instead compliant, unthinking little robots for the machine of industrial society. Much of teaching behavior, in the holy name of Good Grades, could have been designed in a psych laboratory to disorient and shatter the self-confidence of young people, particularly those with ADHD.

Instead, parents and teachers can work together to help modify our learning environments so that emphasis is put on building an enthusiasm for learning, rather than the ability to do short-term rote memory to pass a test. Grades based on the ability to memorize and recite minutiae should be replaced by a simple pass/fail system in which the teacher determines if the student has mastered the topic, understands the material, and can carry that understanding forward into other areas of study and life. In other words, we need to go back to the system that worked so well for thousands of years before Farish decided to become history's most famous lazy teacher.

WHEN PEOPLE DON'T FIT IN

Isolation is one of the most painful emotions a human can experience. The isolation people experience when they lose or are rejected by a lover can lead to suicide and occasionally even murder. The most brutal punishment our prisons can mete out is to put a convict in solitary confinement, inflicting isolation on them for hours, days, or even weeks. Prisoners have become insane from spending extended times in isolation, as have POWs who were isolated in order to break their will.

We humans are social animals. We need others around us, and

we need their approval and friendship. Without these things, our emotional development is stunted, our souls are wounded, and, in some cases, monsters are created. Isolation is the fire on which the human psyche is burned and sometimes destroyed.

Children with ADHD are often socially as well as academically isolated.

The school environment conspires in this by sending them to separate "special" classes and "resource" rooms and labeling them as "attentionally disordered" and "defective." Who wants to have a friend who's defective? Not the average ten-year-old.

When people don't fit in, the results are unpredictable. In some cases, brilliant loners such as Einstein or Hemingway blossom from their isolation—most often when they have supportive parents and an extended family network, and most visibly in times past when schools and social institutions were in many ways more tolerant of ADHD. In other cases, people writhe in social pain for the whole of their lives, only occasionally touching a sense of self-worth and happiness, and only rarely finding another person with whom they can share their isolation. They often struggle with their wounds and isolation their entire lives, sometimes producing creative brilliance, but more often producing a half-lived life full of "what could have been."

The very process of attaching a label that contains the words "disorder" and "deficit" is isolating. It defines a person not only as different, but as inferior, damaged, and broken. Not normal. Different.

For this reason, among others, I prefer to call people with what we call ADHD "Hunters" and people without ADHD "Farmers." These terms are relatively value neutral and, while they acknowledge difference, don't imply inferiority or superiority. This is the beginning of stopping the damage done to children with ADHD, and it can even be retroactively applied (with techniques we'll discuss later) to help adults reinvent their childhood and soothe some of their scars.

A single change in focus can be emancipating; changing the focus of multiple aspects of life can be transformative. Changing grading procedures to focus on mastery, creating school environments that honestly nurture rather than inhibit self-esteem, and shifting perspective to focus on the positive attributes a person with ADHD possesses can make a big difference in the life of your child and in the lives of children for generations to come.

PART 2

Living with ADHD in the Modern World

6

The Beginning of Stigmatization of ADHD

In every one of those little stucco boxes, there's some poor bastard who's never free except when he's fast asleep and dreaming that he's got the boss down the bottom of a well and is bunging lumps of coal at him.

GEORGE ORWELL (1903–1950), BRITISH WRITER, *COMING UP FOR AIR*, 1939

Anyone who has passed through the regular gradations of a classical education, and is not made a fool by it, may consider himself as having had a very narrow escape.

WILLIAM HAZLITT (1778–1830), BRITISH WRITER, "ON THE IGNORANCE OF THE LEARNED"

IN COMMUNITIES OF FARMERS and herders, the most important skills were a strong back, a love of the outdoors, and the ability to chase a wayward animal without tiring. By and large, this held true from the time of the agricultural revolution ten thousand years ago until the Middle Ages. We went from coordinating our activities by nature (the rising and setting sun and the weather) to beginning and ending our work by an artificial measurement devised entirely by the mind of man. This change did not bode well for some of those with ADHD, as it reshaped society in a way that conflicted with their inner sense of the world, a sense that would come to be judged as not accurate, not obedient, and therefore not "normal."

The first known clock was invented around six thousand years ago in China. It worked by passing water through a complex set of containers and pipes, and it marked the hours, days, weeks, and months. It was, however, only a tool of the court astrologers and a toy for the royal family.

In the thirteenth century in Europe, a mechanical clock was invented in the Benedictine monasteries for the purpose of organizing when throughout the day to say prayers. It remained a tool of the monks for almost a hundred years until 1370, when French king Charles V ordered that the churches of Paris disregard their prayer times and instead ring their bells every hour on the hour, as were rung the bells of the royal palace, and that all businesses in Paris must regulate their work hours in accordance with these hourly bells. Some have speculated that the good king was a bit compulsive or anal-retentive, but regardless of the health or neurosis of his motives the result of his order was profound. Over time, the practice of hourly bells had spread throughout Europe, where it is practiced in small towns to this day.

It was the beginning of the tyranny of the timepiece and signaled a significant shift in the way people interacted with the world. It also brought into sharp focus the difficulties people with ADHD's often incoherent sense of time would face as society made these shifts.

Now, a new skill was necessary for success in the workplace: the ability to understand time and conform to the demands of the clock bells. Those ADHD-like individuals—the freethinkers and born independents—now very much found themselves on the outside of workaday society, looking in.

From working by the clock, we moved into the age of the factory. James Watt's 1675 invention of the steam engine and the widespread discovery of coal around Europe fueled huge factories in the eighteenth and nineteenth centuries, opening the doors to the Industrial Revolution. Barber/surgeon Richard Arkwright opened the first chain of factories in Britain in 1780 with twenty cotton-spinning mills across the country. Although most of the workers in his mills were children, Arkwright nonetheless earned a knighthood from the Crown, became fabulously rich, and helped establish a new standard for the normal work environment. By 1800 other entrepreneurs had opened mills and factories in virtually every city in Britain, and the practice quickly jumped across the English Channel to spread through Europe and, from there, to America.

While during the first few decades of the Industrial Revolution factory work was largely the duty of children, as populations in cities swelled, a growing unemployed adult workforce pushed for the elimination of this unfair competition. Unions were formed along the lines of historic trade guilds, and governments were petitioned to bar children from the workplace and establish a minimum wage benchmark.

With this new workplace came a new necessary skill for workers: the ability to perform repetitive tasks for hours at a time. With the centralization of that workplace came other necessary new skills: the ability to follow orders, unite behind management or leadership, and find a political and social slot into which one could fit and then remain in that slot for years. For those with

ADHD who thrive on change (such as Ben Franklin, who had thirty-seven "careers" in his lifetime), this societal shift was a thundering assault.

As power and wealth continued to concentrate into fewer and fewer hands, compliance and obedience came to be seen as desirable social/psychological traits. Those who were not compliant or obedient, particularly to authority figures, were publicly humiliated, flogged, hung, tortured, burned, or executed. Parents were encouraged to beat their children into servility, a practice that appeared as a recommendation in some European childcare manuals as recently as 1944.

The philosophical basis of this child-rearing strategy persists to this day. In 1996 I was interviewed on a nationwide BBC (British Broadcasting Corporation) radio program about ADHD, along with a teacher and a psychologist. The teacher asserted that many of the so-called ADHD children merely had bad attitudes, and the psychologist suggested that poor parenting was the root problem of most of the nation's ADHD children. The main message was to deal with ADHD, just beat them a little harder, shout a little louder, and they'll eventually fall into line.

As mentioned earlier, the majority of the world's money is currently controlled by a small group of corporations and government agencies. Most Americans work for the government or one of fewer than five hundred companies. What's good for General Motors *is,* apparently, what is good for America. And what's good for General Motors is to have compliant, obedient, unquestioning workers—definitely people who are *not* ADHD—and who are educated in such a way as to not have higher aspirations or even the means to reach them, should such ideas flit through their minds from time to time.

This is "normal." It's what we, as a society, have decided is most useful for our cultural survival. It's the standard against which normalcy and abnormality are measured.

This standard, reflected in society and family, is the foundational struggle that creates all other struggles for ADHD children and adults.

7

ADHD as a Response to the Modern World

Man finds nothing so intolerable as to be in a state of complete rest, without passions, without occupation, without diversion, without effort. Then he feels his nullity, loneliness, inadequacy, dependence, helplessness, emptiness.

BLAISE PASCAL (1623–1662), FRENCH PHILOSOPHER
AND MATHEMATICIAN, *PENSÉES*, 1670

HERE'S ANOTHER REFRAMING of ADHD that you may find useful.

The brain, as it develops through childhood, creates millions of neural interconnections as the result of experience. These connections of brain cells and the way in which they're organized largely determine how a child or adult will react to the world in the future. For example, studies reported in *Science News* on September 6, 1997, show that when baby rats are handled by humans for fifteen minutes a day during the first few weeks of life, they are significantly bolder and more adventurous as adults than rats that are not handled by humans. Whether it's the human handling, or the fact that the mother rat licks the handled babies more than the unhandled ones, which input causes this personality trait is a matter of speculation, but the fact remains that experience in early life provides a stage, as it were, for the way later life is experienced and conducted.

Consider the modern child who grows up in front of the television, with images changing and shifting every three to six seconds, camera angles constantly canting and changing, and information flying at an incredibly rapid rate. Even if the information is not particularly useful ("Buy our product!"), it comes fast and furious, with maximal emotional, psychological, and—most importantly—neurological impact. (Advertising agencies are among the most common clients for NLP, hypnosis, and other "deep psychology" trainings.)

The child's brain is wired for rapid response, fine-tuned by video games and interactive toys. Dolls don't just sit there, they talk or wet their pants. Guns fire rays and make rapid, loud noises. The child grows up in an environment of massively high stimulation.

And so the brain becomes wired to handle information rapidly. Bring it on, bring it in, but bring it *fast* is the child's mantra. Masterpiece Theatre on Public Television holds no charm or interest. Each new program or toy must be more stimulating than the last, and the natural world of flowers and grass and trees is only "out there" compared to the immediacy of TV, video games, and high-stim toys.

Then this high-speed child, whose brain has been programmed essentially since birth to respond *fast* to stimuli and demand *new and interesting* input on a continual basis, goes to school.

The teaching methods of our schools have not changed significantly in the past ten generations and in many ways haven't changed in four thousand years. The teacher doesn't jump around the room, cant from side to side, or utter witticisms and entertaining dialogue every twenty seconds. The room doesn't change every few seconds. Instruction isn't interrupted every six to seven minutes with interesting commercials and opportunities to take a bathroom or snack break. Things are static and boring for brains wired for an environment that is constantly changing and therefore stimulating.

I remember driving on the autobahn in Germany, where there is no speed limit. Driving a borrowed Audi, I hit 110 miles an hour, holding the steering wheel with both hands, thrilled and frightened and mostly amazed as Porsches and Mercedes passed me on the left going 120, 130, and as fast as 150 MPH. But my most vivid memory of that drive from Nuremberg to Munich, which I often made during the year I lived in Germany, was the stretch of about twenty miles through a forest pass, where the authorities had imposed a 100 kilometer-per-hour (about 60 MPH) speed limit on the autobahn because of the winding and dangerous mountain roads. It was unbearable! I felt like I was trapped, impatient and fidgety, pushing right to the edge of the 60 MPH as I anticipated the end of the speed zone and the resumption of the (literally) gas-pedal-to-the-floor speeds.

The fast driving had conditioned me to be bored by the slow areas!

Today's child, with a brain conditioned by rapid-fire images from TV, toys, and video games, enters the snail's-paced world of public schools. What's the natural response? "Teach me faster! Stimulate me!" the child may cry.

But the child isn't sufficiently articulate to say such things, so they merely fidget, hoping for a glimmer of stimulation in the lesson, or trying to provide a bit of stimulation by acting out.

And the response of the teacher and the school? "This child isn't fitting in! Something must be wrong!"

As with all reframings, this may have a lot of or a little truth to it. The world of our minds and perceptions is never the objective world, which we are forever prevented from knowing by our lack of mind-reading skills, our lack of x-ray eyes, and our inability to see into an atom or out to the stars. But it may be useful: a new map for the territory of what we call ADHD.

8

If You Have ADHD, Society Needs You

The great challenge which faces us is to assure that, in our society of big-ness, we do not strangle the voice of creativity, that the rules of the game do not come to overshadow its purpose, that the grand orchestration of society leaves ample room for the man who marches to the music of another drummer.

HUBERT H. HUMPHREY (1911–1978), AMERICAN
VICE PRESIDENT, SPEECH ON JUNE 29, 1966

NOVELTY-SEEKING BEHAVIOR is at the core of what we call ADHD, and without novelty societies stop growing. When people stop looking for new experiences and new ways to do things and stop allowing variations in the way humans express their humanness, then culture is at risk of stagnation and eventual death. This is what happened to Japan at one point in its history.

In the 1500s Japan closed itself to the world. For three centuries nobody from any other country was allowed into Japan, and nobody in Japan was allowed out. During this time, referred to as the Meiji Era, Japanese society stagnated. Social institutions changed not at all, and there was virtually no technological advancement. Some literature came out of the period, but even that contained little innovation, no new stylistic modes, and few new insights. The Samurai of the period had permission to kill any person who offended them in any way, so the word "no" was excised from the language and a disconnected, third-person way of speaking became the norm. (Instead of saying, "I don't want to do that," one might say, "It is possible that a person would find many things of interest to do.") Anybody who tried to rebel, innovate, or even stand out from the crowd was mercilessly removed from the gene pool by the Samurai. The phrase, "The nail that sticks up will be hammered down" came to define Japanese culture.

Then, in 1853, British commodore Perry parked his fleet of "Black Ships" off the coast of Japan. He sent emissaries to the Emperor and asked for an audience, saying that he wanted to trade with the Japanese. He was rebuffed. So in his second message he told the emperor that if he wasn't allowed to engage in trade with Japan, he would instead declare war on the nation. The doors opened, and Japanese society underwent, over the next twenty years, one of the most radical transformations it's experienced in the past five centuries.

This is not to say that all that is new is also good. Certainly, there is great value in the traditional and the time-tested. But if societies thrive because of innovation—and most innovation has historically come from the misfits, the not-in-step, and the tangential thinkers—then having a lot of ADHD people in a society may, in fact, contribute to its growth and vibrancy.

Certainly, the experiments of the United States, Australia, and Taiwan indicate this is probably so. All three countries were founded by the expatriates, misfits, and rejects of European and Chinese society. All three have a long tradition of respecting the "outsider" and encouraging innovation. And all three lead the world in developing and promoting new products and new ways of looking at the world.

Societies such as North Korea, where innovation, change, and independence are crushed under the heel of conformity, usually begin to rot within their cultural cores, eventually collapsing under their own weight.

This is an important story to share with your children, if they have ADHD, and to know yourself if you do. You are useful and capable. As Lynn Weiss points out in her brilliant book *A.D.D. and Creativity* (Taylor Publishers), ADHD people have numerous strengths, and our society would be a very different, and much less pleasant and happy, place without them.

PART 3

Healing Memories of a Lifetime with ADHD

9

What Doesn't Kill Us
Makes Us Stronger

*Difficulty, my brethren, is the nurse of greatness—a
harsh nurse, who roughly rocks her foster-children into
strength and athletic proportion.*

WILLIAM CULLEN BRYANT (1794–1878),
AMERICAN WRITER, SPEECH ON DECEMBER 15, 1851

ONE OF THE MOST ENDURING clichés is, "What doesn't kill you
makes you stronger," though this is not an idea that is popular with
people in the recovery movement.

The most common story shared among students of psychology
is that childhood traumas cause adult neuroses. In many cases, of
course, this is true. On the other hand, there are also numerous stories of mass murderers and generally nutso people who came from
"perfectly normal" backgrounds, as well as people who survived hell-
ish childhoods to become productive and happy members of society.

Nobody escapes childhood unscathed. In our culture, children
often behave—even unintentionally—in ways that are notoriously
cruel, and if a child isn't tortured or maimed emotionally by their parents, this torment is often inflicted by their peers. It's not just people
in therapy who have horror stories to tell about their childhoods: it's

just about everybody. It's true that not everybody was beaten, burned, or starved as altogether too many children are in America every year. But little kids don't have a lifetime's experience to judge reality by either—they don't know that one particular type of hurt is qualitatively worse or better than another. One child may be psychically scarred by a sharp word from a friend, whereas another is hurt by a parent's blow with a belt. Both have—in their own minds—sustained wounds. One of the most universal stories that people with ADHD will tell you is how they were wounded by the experience of their school years, be it from difficulties with teachers and structure or impulsiveness causing social crises. Though some might not judge these experiences as life altering, it only matters how the person who lived them views them.

Interestingly, studies show that it's often not so much the type of wound inflicted on a child that will determine their later course in life as it is the story they tell themselves about the wound. *The Resilient Self*, by Steven Wolin and Sybil Wolin, tells of a thirty-year-long study of highly at-risk children from the poorest migrant neighborhoods of Kauai, Hawaii, which found that when children with extremely difficult and painful lives grow up, those among them who had adjusted themselves to the adversity of their childhood often have stronger internal psychological resilience than those children who grew up "unscathed" in normal middle-class families. Those who told themselves they were powerless and thought of themselves as victims were the most damaged; those who decided the "fault" was with their abuser(s) and not themselves often actually became stronger internally as a result of their difficulties.

What this study and others show is that we are not automatically destined to have lives of failure and difficulty just because we had unfortunate childhood experiences. As Wendy Kaminer points out in her book *I'm Dysfunctional, You're Dysfunctional*, which was recently cited in another study in *Psychology Today*, over 70 percent of the children of severe alcoholics have no problem with alcohol whatsoever. The links, while certainly happening from time to time, are not automatic.

Unfortunately, popular culture emphasizes the pain and damage that a difficult childhood can cause. TV and radio shows, self-help groups, and magazine and newspaper advice columns go on at length about the importance of spending hours with a therapist reliving painful experiences of youth in order to "heal." In many ways, we've become a society obsessed with sickness, spending large parts of our lives in dubious therapies trying to resolve problems that could instead have been reframed as learning and strengthening experiences.

Research shows that the pain and wounds of growing up in difficult circumstances—including growing up an ADHD Hunter in a Farmer's world—can be grist for the mill of our lives. These experiences can be revisited later in life in ways that transform them, and *quickly*.

Understanding that reality is one of the most important of the techniques at the core of this book. It's the basis of how you can change your life, if you grew up with ADHD, and how you can help your child change their perception of life and ADHD.

10

Finding Your Calm and Powerful Center

Know thyself.

The self-explorer, whether he wants to or not, becomes the explorer of everything else. He learns to see himself, but suddenly, provided he was honest, all the rest appears, and it is as rich as he was, and, as a final crowning, richer.

ELIAS CANETTI (1905–1994), AUSTRIAN
WRITER AND PHILOSOPHER, *THE SECRET
HEART OF THE CLOCK*, 1987

THIS IDEA MAY SEEM a bit metaphysical to you at first, but if you follow the information presented here, you'll discover that it's eminently practical.

There is a calm and powerful center in each of us and in each of our children. It's the place that existed even before we were born; some would say even before we were conceived. Some books and schools of psychology or self-help refer to touching or stepping into this place as "centering." Others talk about "finding your bliss" or touching nirvana, samadhi, enlightenment, or satori.

While these are universal concepts, they're of particular import to people wounded by growing up with ADHD in our modern Farmer society.

An interesting way to understand it is to imagine that there was a time when all your needs were met and you were perfectly happy, floating in Mom's amniotic fluid. Life was good. Then you were born, and suddenly life wasn't so good: your stomach told you it was hungry, your butt said it was chafed, your skin was too cold or warm, and on and on.

In response to these *needs*, you developed new *behaviors*. Crying was one of the first, although it was accompanied by waving arms and legs, shaking, kicking, and other physical motions. As you grew and learned to manipulate your physical environment, you began to pull, push, crawl, walk, and eventually talk as ways to express your needs.

Every time a new need arose, a new part of your brain/mind was activated as a resource to meet that need. One part took responsibility for getting the diapers changed, another for getting fed, another for getting hugs from Mom, and so on.

As you went through life, thousands of parts split off and took on an independent responsibility to handle particular crises, needs, desires, and problems. Very often these parts were momentary loci of focused energy and attention, and when they were finished with their job, they simply dissolved back into the totality of the "center," which is you. Others were responsible for ongoing and lifelong needs, such as the need to be fed or the need for affection or the need to protect the body or personality. They took on relatively independent lives of their own.

Every adult and every kid has different "parts" that they show to different people and use in different circumstances. The part you or your child brings to the fore when you're having a fight is very different from the part in charge when you're falling in love (at least if you're like most people), and both are quite different from the part that takes charge when you're applying for a job, speaking with a teacher, or fighting for something you believe in. We all have these various parts that we can move to the front when needed. The difference between this and multiple personality disorder (MPD) is that in MPD, each part takes over completely, blocking out of conscious awareness all other parts. In a normally functioning person, no matter which part is in the fore, there is still an overall sense of continuous identity.

These various parts have coalesced and emerged over the years; they are learned skills that now take responsibility for handling certain parts of our lives.

The goal of each of these parts is to return you or your child to that calm center you once knew so intimately very early in your life. No matter what the function may be—nourishment, defense, affection, aggression, or anything else—the *goal* of that function is to return you to a whole, centered state.

Another way to say this is that the goal of each of these parts is to share in consciousness. While they may also serve to maintain and protect other parts and functions, their ultimate goal is to partake in a slice of the life of the human being. To touch consciousness . . . that calm center.

DYSFUNCTIONAL PARTS

However, life is not so uncomplicated. In order to meet a need, a part may have to handle a dozen different actions. To get fed, it may have to deal with issues of finance, choices about types of and places for food, social interactions associated with food, and a whole range of other things. It will probably have to cooperate or negotiate with other parts—the parts that control making money, for example, or handle social skills.

If life were simple, a part could simply emerge, get a need met, and then dissolve back into the center. As it is, parts often take on a life of their own. They sometimes forget their original purpose and run through our lifetimes as if on autopilot, performing some secondary or tertiary task that no longer has any apparent connection to the original need/goal that caused the part to take on an existence of its own.

When this happens, we have what some call neurotic behaviors. People get into ruts, repeating over and over behaviors that have no apparent purpose and don't seem to serve their needs at all. While those behaviors may not serve the person's overall needs, however, they do (or did at one time) serve some need, somewhere. If they didn't, they never would have emerged in the first place.

That need, however, may have been long ago satisfied in some other way. The first (or second, or third) part that emerged to satisfy the need was simply never informed that its job was no longer necessary. And it keeps on trying, over and over again, in ways that don't at all work, to get the need fulfilled.

HOW FREUD WAS HALF-RIGHT

Sigmund Freud had a patient come to his practice with a case of paralysis. Freud was then developing a theory about personality that assumed most aspects of behavior originated in childhood, so he walked this woman through her past until their discussion caused her to remember a previously forgotten incident of childhood trauma. When she remembered this, her paralysis went away.

This case (and a few other similar ones) caused Freud to hypothesize that remembering childhood traumas will cure the neurotic adult behaviors that have resulted from them. An entire school of therapy emerged from this—Freudian psychotherapy—which seemed to work quite well for hysterical paralysis, a common condition among women in Freud's day.

What Freud overlooked, however, was the mechanism at work. It apparently didn't occur to him that when the woman remembered her childhood trauma, she may also have done some processing of that memory, probably in just a matter of seconds. Perhaps she forgave the others involved in her pain. Maybe she decided, looking back with the viewpoint of an adult, that it wasn't such a big deal. Or she realized that in the intervening years, she'd developed other ways to deal with such trauma and could apply one of those to the memory, instantly resolving it. Whatever it was, she had to have done *something* with that memory.

What most commonly happens to Freudian therapy patients is that they're walked back into old, painful memories and then have to describe the content of those memories to the therapist. In order to do that, they have to increase the contrast and brightness, turn still pictures into movies, and listen to the sound. They change the submodalities, often intensifying the memories and increasing their power to hurt and haunt. They then move the memories from behind them in time to in front of them. The memories that were once in the past now become an ongoing part of the present and even color the future (more about this when we talk about transforming your timelines in chapter 13.) The predictable result is that the process of therapy itself can be traumatizing, essentially forcing the patient to repeatedly reinflict on themselves the old pains, which they would just as soon be done with.

There's also a voyeuristic element to this type of therapy, which is disconcerting to some observers of the psychological scene. Freud was admittedly the quintessential voyeur. He saw himself as blazing new frontiers into the human mind, and therefore the content of that mind was vitally important to him. He believed it to be a primary key to understanding how everything worked together.

What we've learned since then is that content isn't nearly as important as the way content is stored (submodalities) and responded to (stories we tell ourselves). (In the next chapter we'll talk about how this can be used to heal people from the pain they've experienced from growing up with ADHD in an ADHD-hostile world.) Because of this, it's entirely possible—and, indeed, today quite common—for good therapists to work with patients to cure phobias, neurotic behaviors, and a whole host of other "psychological ailments" *without ever once having to know or listen to the details of content.*

We do, however, live in a culture heavily influenced by nearly two thousand years of the rule of the Catholic Church. And that Church taught that one method for people to be "saved" is to first tell all of their secret sins to a high official of the Church, who would then, speaking on behalf of God, instruct the penitent as to which particular ceremonies or prayers or deeds to perform, or how much money to give to the Church, in order to have God forgive the sins. Back in the old days, the Catholic Church ended up with the blackmail scoop on *everybody,* a fact that was not lost on Church officials (or the "leaders" of the countries they unofficially ruled) for centuries.

Out of this tradition, which served well the traditional religious and political power structures of our culture, came the popular myth that "confession is good for the soul." In some cases, this is no doubt the case, particularly when that confession gives people a lever to process their own internal pain and change the submodalities associated with a particular memory. In other cases, however, and particularly in those types of "therapy" where old and forgotten "sins" are ferreted out, confession can be merely the perpetual reopening of a once-healed scab or even the fulfillment of a voyeuristic need on the part of the therapist.

So Freud was right in his belief that some neurotic behavior has its origins in some past time. Where he was wrong was in assuming that by simply remembering it, and spilling the contents of it to a therapist, it would be healed.

Instead, it is necessary to reconnect the part that controls the behavior back to its original goal—that centered place within.

RECONNECTING YOUR PARTS TO THEIR CENTER

While it was once believed that the entire home of the mind was in the physical organ of the brain, recent research is challenging this theory. The heart, stomach, liver, and small intestine are among a few of the organs that have been discovered to have extensive neural networks and to host measurable amounts of neurotransmitters that were previously believed to be the sole province of the brain. Similarly, some heart surgeons have reported that their transplant patients underwent personality changes, even developing some of the personality characteristics of the now-dead person who donated their new heart. In some cases, heart recipients have even experienced "memories" from the lives of their heart donors.

This is leading to a redefinition of the nature and presumed seat of consciousness. While the brain is still acknowledged as a critical organ in the process, it's no longer believed to be the only part involved. It's looking more and more like the entire body—virtually every cell—may be (it's a field fraught with controversy) in one way or another interconnected with the process of what we call consciousness.

This fits in well with the discovery, made a few decades ago by Milton Erickson and others, that our various personality parts have not only a psychological home, but a physical one too. They usually take up residence somewhere in the body, leading to chronic tension in a particular muscle or aches and pains in various parts of the body. If you ask a person where the part of them that controls a particular behavior—for example, their smoking, overeating, or constant complaining—lives, they'll usually be able to name or point to a particular part of their body. "It's in my stomach," they'll say, or "I feel it as a tension in my neck." It could be anywhere; sometimes it's even hanging out somewhere near but not in the body. I've had people describe a part as existing "two feet in front of my head," or "just behind the small of my back." Most often, though, it's in the body.

GETTING IN CONTACT WITH A PART

To illustrate this, I'll tell the story of a friend who'd expressed curiosity about this process. We'd known this woman for several years, and while she was endearing in many ways, she had one obnoxious part of her personality: she constantly interrupted people, often with complaints. Nothing was ever right. The food was too cold, too hot, too salty, too sweet. The room was too bright. Her clothes weren't fashionable enough. This friend was too judgmental; that one was too dumb. And on and on. It seemed that this woman's life revolved around her interrupting and complaining, and all of her friends knew it. After reading a book about ADHD, she'd come to conclude that this was "just the way people with ADHD are," but nonetheless she had hope of changing her behaviors.

So she asked me if it was possible to get rid of her lifelong interrupting and complaining behavior, and I said that we could give it a try.

We were driving down highway I-75 in Atlanta, on our way to the Sunday morning church services downtown. We had about fifteen minutes more driving to go—I guessed it would be enough time. She was in the back seat, and I could see her in the rearview mirror.

"Relax and close your eyes," I said, "and just let yourself float down into the seat." I checked the mirror and could see her relax.

"Now," I said, "the part of you that is responsible for your interrupting and complaining behavior—that thing that you believe defines your ADHD. Where does it usually hang out in your body?"

"That's an interesting question," she said. "I never thought of it as a separate part." There was a moment of a puzzled look on her face, and then she smiled. "Oh! Here it is, in my stomach."

"Good," I said. "Now, put your hand on that part and thank it for all the years that it has been with you and helped you."

"But I don't like that behavior!" she said.

"You mean that *some* parts of you don't like that behavior. But the part that is controlling it has been doing that for you for years, and, believe me, it's been doing it because it thinks that it's the best thing for you. Every part of you is working, in its own way, for your benefit and good. *Every* part, including this one. So please thank that part for all its diligent work and efforts on your behalf all these years. Just do it silently, in your head, speaking to that part in your stomach."

"OK," she said, and spent a moment quietly as I continued to drive. The traffic was light, and it was a sparkling bright winter morning; we were beginning to enter the outskirts of the city. After about a minute, she said, "I think it's happy that I've acknowledged it."

"Good," I said. "Now, I'd like you to ask that part what it has been trying to accomplish all these years by its complaining. What is it trying to do? What is its goal?"

This is the first step beyond Freud, who assumed that "neurotic" parts came into being as the result of repressed trauma but had no specific purpose, or if they did have a goal, it was a purely defensive one. Instead, I was assuming that this part had a *positive* purpose, a specific goal. It was trying to accomplish something. However, odds are that over the years it had also forgotten the specifics of that goal in attempts to come up with new and more complex behaviors to reach the goal.

"It says that it wants things 'to be all right,'" she said. "That's amazing—it was almost like I could hear a voice inside of me. As soon as I asked the question, I heard the answer."

"Good," I said. "Now, thank that part for working so hard to have things be all right over these many years. That's a noble purpose, and it's worked very hard on your behalf. It deserves to be thanked."

"It says, 'You're welcome,'" she said and laughed.

"Good," I said, repeating again the word that I was using to anchor our friend's process and encourage her. "But I'm sure that having 'everything be all right' isn't the deepest goal of this part. I suspect that it has a much more important mission to play in your life, and it has for years. So ask it to imagine that everything *is* all right and, if that were the case, what would be an even deeper goal?"

"It doesn't want people to fight," she said.

"Good," I said. "Please thank that part for helping to keep people from fighting." I paused for a moment until she nodded, indicating she'd thanked her part. "Now, ask it if nobody was fighting, what would be an even deeper goal?"

"It wants me to be loved," she said, her voice softening.

"Good," I said. "That's a very important goal, and that part of you has worked tirelessly for years to help accomplish it, and so you can thank it for that effort. But I'll bet there's an even more important goal, a deeper goal, which that part has had as a more important work all these years. So ask it, 'If you were totally loved and that was completely taken care of, what is an even deeper goal?'"

"To *be* love," she replied immediately.

"Good," I said. "That's very good. Thank that part for helping you to be love all these years. And now ask that part, 'What's a deeper goal than to be love?'"

I was keeping a careful eye on our friend in the rearview mirror. In the seconds after I asked that question, she relaxed so completely she settled another few inches back in her seat. Her face lit up with a beatific smile. She looked ecstatic.

"What is it?" I said.

She sighed happily, then said, "There are no words. I'm surrounded by light and awash in love. No words . . ." Her voice trailed off.

She had reached her centered place, what is referred to by Connierae and Tamara Andreas as her core.* This is the place at the center of her being, what some may call her soul or her enlightenment. It's the place that her complaining-behavior part had been trying to reach all these years through the technique of complaining. It's the wellspring from which the part had arisen, and now we could wash it over all the various components of that part ("be all right," "people don't fight," "be loved," "be love") so that it didn't have barriers between itself and that centered place any longer.

"Good," I said. "Now, ask that part to fill the experience of wanting to 'be love' with that light you're now experiencing. And ask it, when it does this, what it thinks now about the need to 'be love.'"

She smiled. "It doesn't need to work at being love any more, because it *is* love."

"Good," I said. "Now, ask it, if it had that light all the time, if it was always available in all circumstances, how that would make it feel about the need to be loved."

---

*A process similar to this is thoroughly detailed in the Andreases' book *Core Transformation*. There are also references to this type of work in various works about Milton Erickson and in books about NLP by Richard Bandler and John Grinder.

"It doesn't need to be loved. It is love."

"Good! Now, ask it how having full-time access to that light would transform its desire to not have people fight."

"It wouldn't matter," she said. "They could fight or not, it doesn't matter. I don't have to get involved."

"Good! And how would it change its desire to have things be all right?"

She laughed softly. "Everything *is* all right."

"Good," I said, now preparing to go for the top of the mushroom, the visible and persistent and annoying behavior that had driven this woman for years. "Now, ask it how having that light available to it all the time changes its desire to complain about things."

She sighed pleasantly and said, "It doesn't need to complain any more. Everything is fine."

"Good," I said. "Please thank that part for all the work it's done all these years to help you find that light. If it weren't for its persistent efforts, you wouldn't have done this process and touched that center of love and light within yourself. And then you can open your eyes."

She sat silently for a minute or two as I took the exit ramp and began to drive through the city streets of downtown Atlanta. When she finally opened her eyes, she said, "That was amazing."

The amazing part to me, though, was that I've never, since that day, heard our friend complain about anything. Two weeks later, she was walking with Louise and me around the lake we lived on, north of Atlanta. "How's the interrupting and complaining behavior?" I asked.

She gave me a blank look, as if I'd asked her the atomic weight of zinc. "Huh?"

"Your complaining, your ADHD? We worked on it in the car?"

"Oh, yeah," she said, suddenly recalling. "Wow. I don't think I've interrupted anybody with a complaint in weeks. I left that behind entirely."

Wow, indeed.

You can do this with yourself, and you can do it with your children. If you encounter resistance, just stop and try another time or another way.*

---

*There's a lot more detail on this type of technique to be found in the excellent book *Core Transformation* by Connierae and Tamara Andreas.

11

Reconstructing the Past

*We are able to find everything in our memory, which
is like a dispensary or chemical laboratory in which
chance steers our hand sometimes to a soothing drug and
sometimes to a dangerous poison.*

MARCEL PROUST (1871–1922), FRENCH WRITER,
IN SEARCH OF LOST TIME

DIFFERENT TYPES OF MEMORIES—regardless of how anchored in
reality or fantasy they may be—are stored in our brains in different ways. These forms of storage involve the five sensory *modalities*
(sight, smell, hearing, taste, feeling) and the subtle gradations of each
sense (such as color, brightness, or contrast for the visual modality).
These gradations are referred to as *submodalities*. This method of
storage is true for both adults and children, and this NLP concept
can be used to heal the sometimes painful memories brought about
by a lifetime of ADHD.

One of the ways our brain organizes information is according to the way it's stored. Our senses pick up something in the
outside world—say we see an insect fly by. That's an objective
"thing" that we've "seen." However, before that image makes its
way to our conscious brain, it's processed by other parts of the
mind and tweaked and tuned. If it's a bug that frightens us, per-

haps a wasp, then the mind sees it as being bigger and in sharper contrast than it really is. Other objects in the picture—the background, buildings, grass, whatever—become more distant, dull, and perhaps less colorful. The mind may increase the volume of the sound associated with the wasp and also attach a feeling to the image—probably a variation on what we interpret as fear or panic, a feeling felt, perhaps, in the pit of the stomach or a trembling of the hands.

Some of the submodalities that we commonly use to experience reality and store memory include:

Visual: color or black and white, contrast, size, bordered or not, moving or still, brightness, graininess, distance from us, associated or disassociated (do we see the scene as we saw it, or do we see ourselves in it in our memory), focus, detail, texture, perspective, dimensionality (flat or 3-D), proportion

Auditory: loudness, tonality, distance, pitch, melody, inflection, location, tempo, duration

Gustatory: salty, sweet, spicy, musty, bitter, familiar (associated with particular named food or taste), delicate

Olfactory: strong, faint, intermittent, familiar, unique, musty, moist, damp, mildewy

Kinesthetic: hard, soft, cool, warm, sharp, electric, intensity, duration, speed, location

CHANGING "REALITY"

Now here's the amazing part. If you know what modalities and submodalities you use to store a particular type of memory—whether that memory is happy, sad, hopeful, afraid, neutral, or whatever—then you can adjust the memories you have of the past to change their emotional feel. You can do this yourself or help your child through the exercise in order to change the emotional feel of harmful memories associated with ADHD.

For example, think of a memory of something you did in the recent past, such as brushing your teeth last night. Mentally list the quality of the submodalities. Your list may look something like mine: I see a still picture in black and white, without a lot of contrast or detail, associated (I can see the mirror and sink, but not myself), no border, 3-D, about two feet square, about twenty feet away from me, and I can hear the sound of the water running and taste the mint of the toothpaste. If I concentrate on it, I can remember (or imagine) the feeling of the toothbrush on my gums and the smell of the toothpaste.

The feelings I associate with that memory are pretty neutral. Boredom may be the best way to describe it. It's something I do every night.

Now, imagine a control panel just below the image you've created, or wherever you'd like it to be, with dials and levers that you can use to change the various submodalities.

Reach out and change a few of the submodalities, and see how things change! When I move the picture from black and white to color, I suddenly feel curious and interested in the process of brushing my teeth. It seems fascinating. If I turn up the volume, I become uneasy. As I increase the mint taste, I feel more awake.

Nobody knows why this works the way it does. One theory is that the brain stores information holographically, rather than digitally, so the brain "sees" its own storage capacity as a three-dimensional space. Because we experience the world through our senses, it makes sense that we'd also organize the mechanism for storing the information about our experience of the world along sensory lines as well. When something is put into a particular space, it acquires the sensory nature of that space, since sensory signals are how we experience the world.

So when a memory is put into the "boring" category in our brain, it becomes (in my case, but everybody is different) black and white still pictures. When the submodalities are adjusted and the picture is turned into a color movie, it doesn't just change the emotional quality of the memory: it actually causes it to interconnect with or slide to a different storage place in the holographic brain.

If you took that boring memory and changed the submodalities so that the emotions associated with it changed, and then you left it that way, you probably have permanently changed the nature of that memory. If you do it a few times, you will definitely permanently (until you tweak the submodalities again) change the memory, as long as your deep unconscious believes it to be valuable to you. As you ask your children how they store their memories, you'll discover the types of submodalities they associate with particular states.

Using the toothbrushing or other "boring" memory, you now know how you or your child encodes and stores boring memories. Do a reality check by bringing up a few other boring memories, and see if they're the same. Once you've determined the common submodality elements among all your boring memories, note the submodality details. This is important information for you to remember—you may even want to write it down.

CRITICAL SUBMODALITIES

There's also a concept known as a *critical submodality*. This is the submodality that has the ability to shift others, probably the primary hook into the place in the brain hologram where the memory is stored. As you're going through the various submodalities, changing each one a bit in one way and then another, turning up and then down the brightness, volume, and so on, you'll notice that there is generally one particular one—it could be anything from volume to contrast to smell to brightness to anything else—that causes the entire picture to "change" and creates a sudden shift in the feelings associated with that memory. That submodality is the *critical submodality,* and once you know what your critical submodalities are, you can do this process much quicker.

One of the most common and most powerful critical submodalities is location. When you move a picture from where it is (for example, in front of you and to the right, about four feet away) to some other place (for example, to the front of you, up slightly above the eyes, only a foot away) it often dramatically changes its impact.

CHANGING OUR STORIES AND THOSE OF OUR CHILDREN

Everybody's had the experience of seeing two different people react to the same thing in different ways. Say an insult to two different children, and you'll get two different responses. One child may become indignant, or hurt, or angry. Another may think it a joke or turn it into a witticism and throw it back at you. One person, getting cut off in traffic by a reckless teenager, will yell and scream and wave their fist and lay on their horn. Another will simply slow down and let the teenager have some space. It's a fact of life that different people react to different situations in different ways and that the same person is capable of reacting to the same stimuli in a variety of different ways.

There have been times in your life when you and your children have decided—chosen—how to react to things. In order to make this choice, you may have repeated to yourself over and over again a particular saying or story, such as, "They're just a jerk," or "This isn't really worth worrying about." There have been times when you could have been hurt or wounded by somebody's unthinking behavior, and instead you chose to simply be amused by it or to ignore it.

There have been times when you took control of the stories you told yourself about the meaning of events, people, and things. If you think back and look for one of those times, you'll probably discover that there's a feeling of personal empowerment associated with that memory.

Now, examine that memory for its submodalities. Unless your brain is wired in a very unusual way, you'll discover that there are some submodalities that are the same and some that are different. Don't fiddle with the submodalities of this memory at the moment, as it's a memory of strength and power, and you want to keep as many of those around as you can. But do make a note of the submodalities associated with that memory. How bright is it? How far away? Is it in color or black and white? Is it a movie or a still picture?

Now, pull up a memory of a time that was moderately uncomfortable, perhaps a bit embarrassing or whatever is "not a big deal" but "something to avoid" for you. Notice its submodalities.

Now, use your control panel to change the submodalities of the uncomfortable picture to be the same as those of a time when you felt bored or nonplussed about the event, such as brushing your teeth. Notice that we are not dealing with content here—you don't need to move the car or house from picture A into picture B. We're just dealing with the submodalities, the qualitative details of the picture: the sound, taste, smell, and touch of the memory.

If you're like most people, you'll have just changed the emotional charge of the memory from one of discomfort to one of boredom. What a useful skill! Try it with your child—you can always "put things back the way they were" if you hit an uncomfortable submodality. This can also be a useful way of changing the emotional state a child has associated with a particular teacher or topic.

MOVING INTO THE FUTURE

Now, imagine something you have to do in the near future that you don't feel particularly good or bad about. Imagine some small job or detail other than the toothbrushing or whatever that you've been using as your calibration standard up to now. Notice when you bring up your imagination of that job that it probably shares the submodality qualities of your memories of past boring or no-big-deal events. If it's different, it probably at least shares a critical submodality.

Now, use your control panel to adjust the submodalities of that future imagination to be the same as those of your "power" memory. Notice how you can move into a future event a feeling of empowerment, strength, or whatever you prefer.

This use of submodalities is widely known in the advertising industry, although it's rarely mentioned outside the circles of Madison Avenue. During the Bush/Dukakis campaign, for example, the Bush campaign used some folks who know about these technologies to develop ads that always showed Michael Dukakis in black and white with a frame around him and George Bush always in full-screen color. Other Republican ads showed pictures of "nice things" like kids on swings or happy family gatherings in color and full screen, creating that submodality anchor for feeling good. Other ads showed "Negro criminals" (to use a phrase from an outraged Black TV commentator at the time to describe Willy Horton and others who were depicted in the ads) in black and white with a border around them. The graininess, contrast, brightness, and background sounds were carefully controlled to be identical when Willy Horton or Michael Dukakis was on the screen, and then differently identical when George Bush and the idealized American family were on the screen. Voters "knew in their hearts" who was the man for them. The practice is not, of course, limited to political advertising; it's just more obvious and easy to spot there. But it underlies virtually all television advertising now, as these technologies are well known in the TV world.

Similarly, filmmakers mark out the emotional high points of a film. In a horror film, for example, the viewer is trained in the first few scenes as to what music and visual production values (submodalities) mean "Danger!" "Look out!" and "Run! We're all gonna die!" These same anchors are then used in each following scene, and they gain strength each time they're used until the movie doesn't even have to have a threatening scene on camera—only a grainy picture, with quick shots zooming in and out, and a particular music in the background—to get everybody in the theater squirming in their seats.

Using the knowledge of submodalities, you can help your child (or yourself) associate positive-feeling submodalities with things that need to get done (like homework). And you'll find yourself starting to be aware of the subtle effect that anchors, locations, and submodalities have on how you and your child experience and can take control of the experience of life.

12

Shedding Fears and Phobias

What our eyes behold may well be the text of life but one's meditations on the text and the disclosures of these meditations are no less a part of the structure of reality.

WALLACE STEVENS (1879–1955), AMERICAN POET, "THREE ACADEMIC PIECES," 1947

GROWING UP WITH ADHD is often a process that leaves scars that take the form of fears and phobias. Certain situations may cause certain emotions to arise, but those emotions can be altered by changing one's body language. Fear of school or test taking is one of the most common scenarios; given how tough our Farmer school system can be to children with ADHD, this of course makes perfect sense. To combat this, knowing how you access information can help you in stressful moments when you're struggling to think. It's possible to shed these fears yourself and help your child shed them, go beyond fears of test taking or public speaking or just about anything reasonable, and move into a brighter and more powerful future. Much of this is possible through the power to alter how the mind perceives the world and the situations that cause us distress.

ACCESSING EMPOWERED STATES OF BEING

In an earlier chapter, I mentioned how we store memories in different locations of the brain, usually associating them with particular emotional states. This type of state-dependent learning was first demonstrated back in the 1950s, when college psychology students were broken out into two classes. One class was given enough booze to get them thoroughly drunk; the other class was sober. Both were taught some new and somewhat difficult material.

When the students were sober the next day, they were tested on the material. To nobody's surprise, the drunk students didn't learn as well or remember as much of the material. But then came the surprise: they got the drunk-learning students drunk and gave them the test again. This time they scored significantly better than they had when sober. If you learn something when you're drunk, it turns out you'll remember it more easily when you're drunk again. (The study was reproduced in 1983 and published by the National Institutes of Health.)

The same is true of things you learn when you're angry, bored, happy, in love, upset, or under the influence of drugs. Our minds are organized for state-dependent learning.

Wouldn't it be interesting if there were some sort of an external indicator that you could hang around a person's neck that would tell you when they were accessing what states? If it could tell you when they were remembering a picture, hearing a sound, or experiencing feelings?

It turns out that just such an indicator exists, and NLP has mapped it.

To some extent, it's a person's entire body. To a highly specific degree, though, it's their eyes.

The eyes are a part of the brain. I remember when I learned that in biology and thought, "No, this can't be true. The eyes are an independent sensory organ." But our professor made it quite clear that the eyes are an extension of the brain, just like the thalamus or hypothalamus or inner ear. They're a seamless part of the nervous system, which is run from the brain. They develop from the brain during fetal development, protruding through the skull to pop out of the front of the face. They're the only external part of the brain: a window, as it were, into the human nervous system.

And the eyes tell us what a person's brain is doing.

When a person facing you looks up and to your right, they're probably accessing a visual memory. If they look up and to your left, they're probably creating a visual image, an imagination. When their eyes look sideways and to your right, they're probably remembering a sound or voice; when they look sideways and to your left, they're imagining a sound. When they look down and to your right, they're probably talking to themselves; and when they look down and to your left, they're accessing feelings, emotions, or tactile sensations. (About half of left-handed people are wired exactly opposite of this, as are about 5 percent of right-handed persons.) Everybody is just a bit different. Rather than memorizing the list, it's always best to calibrate with the person first by asking them questions that would cause them to access a visual memory or imagination.

Try this exercise. Sit down in front of your child or some other person and ask them a few questions that to answer they'd have to access these different states. Here are some examples: What color is the carpet in your car? Can you feel your toes when you wiggle them? How would you describe your best friend's voice? Can you imagine what it would sound like if your best friend talked backwards? What would your bedroom look like if it were painted purple and the floor were covered with feathers? When you ask yourself questions, what are they usually about?

Notice how their eyes move.

This knowledge gives you a new way to make conversations interesting! Just ask questions, and watch people's eyes. No matter how boring they may be, you'll probably find the motion of their eyes fascinating, because it tells you so much about what's going on inside them. It can even be an informal lie detector.

For example, when a person is describing a "real situation" but is looking up and to your left, they may actually be imagining the situation and describing to you their hallucinated visual image. We call this lying. To determine if this is what's happening, calibrate. Ask the person a question you both know the answer to, such as, "Where did you park your car tonight?" Notice where their eyes go. If they're up and to your right just before they answer, then you know that when they go up and to the left, they're most likely making something up.

If you want to make or find a mental picture but are having difficulty doing so, try looking up. If you want to remember or experience a feeling, try looking down and to your right. Want to locate a sound? Look from side to side.

While most of the time eye motion tells us what's going on inside the brain, it's also possible to reverse the process by directing the eyes and posture to change.

Psychologist William James pioneered this long ago when he pointed out that most people think that body posture reflects emotional states. A person walking along all hunched over is most likely feeling poorly, perhaps inadequate or depressed or unhappy. A person walking with their spine straight and chin up is probably feeling pretty good about life.

But James said you can reverse the process. If you're feeling depressed, he suggested that you try standing up straight, taking a deep breath, and looking up and ahead instead of down. The very act of adjusting your posture will alter your brain's neurochemistry, changing your emotional state.

Begin to catalog your postures and the corresponding emotional states. Notice how you can shift states by changing your posture and which postures produce the most rapid and noticeable changes. This is the beginning of taking charge of your own neurochemistry, and it can be applied to many of the "typical ADHD" behaviors that are most often treated with drugs, such as a lack of motivation, constant anxiety (often exploding into full-blown phobias), or emotional reactiveness. It's also a process that's relatively easy to teach to children, so they can control their own emotional states with greater ease.

MAKING YOUR OWN MOVIES

Richard Bandler, who with John Grinder first developed NLP, taught me a "fast phobia cure" technique, which is also in several of his books, including *The Structure of Magic*. The system has been shown in thousands of demonstrations all over the world to cure—really and permanently make go away—phobias of all sorts, from fears of spiders to elevators to public speaking. At a training I attended taught by Bandler, a woman who was a writer for one of London's largest newspapers presented herself. She had such a fear of public speaking, she said, that she was incapable of standing up in front of four or five of her peers to make a presentation at the newspaper where she worked. She didn't stand up and tell us this because she was too frightened. She sat in her seat, hunched over, and told it to the person next to her who related it to the class. Bandler took this terrified woman and walked her through the process I'm about to lay out here. It took five minutes. The transformation was so dramatic that one of London's largest TV stations came to cover her five-minute speech to over one hundred and fifty people on the seventh day of the training. This works, and since "anxiety disorders" are so often part and parcel of a lifetime of ADHD, it can be a very useful tool for ADHDers.

Sit down in a quiet place, and close your eyes. Imagine you're in a movie theater, sitting in a comfortable seat in one of the front rows. The screen in front of you is blank.

Now, float up out of your body, leaving it sitting in that front row, and comfortably drift up to the upper balcony. There, you'll find a remote control device that runs the movie, which you can operate with your mind or your hand.

From your safe place way back in the upper balcony, look down at yourself sitting in the front row. That "you" is looking up at the screen. Now, turn on a still frame, a single picture, of yourself in the situation where you're normally phobic, just before you begin to feel the phobic feeling. Make it a color slide. Then push a button on the control panel and have the movie roll forward through the entire phobic experience, all the way through to the other end, where it's all over and you're feeling OK again. At the end of the movie, freeze that frame on the screen. (If at any time watching the movie becomes too uncomfortable, you can move the screen away, make it smaller, or stop or slow down the movie.)

Now, turn the freeze-framed picture on the screen to black and white.

Float down into your body in the front row; then, body and all, float up into the picture on the screen. Fully associate with the picture; that is, be inside the picture. Look around, and see what you see, hear what you hear, feel what you feel, although it's all in black and white.

Now, run the movie backwards, with all the sounds going backwards, making Donald Duck noises, all the way to the beginning. Let it go jerkily and crazily, the way old-time movies did when they ran backwards.

When you get back to the beginning of the movie, freeze-frame it again and step out of the screen, then float back to your seat in the front row. Look at the black-and-white picture for a moment, then let the screen go white.

Usually, the first run of this wipes out most of the phobia. Imagine yourself in a phobic situation, and see how you feel about it—odds are your feelings will have changed significantly. If there is any lingering phobic feeling, repeat the process.

Many children are "phobic" about school, a particular class, or a particular teacher. Our system seems set up to cause this, particularly for children with ADHD. Even though these are very mild phobias, often really verging on the "I dislike that" to the "I hate that" spectrum, there's usually a significant element of fear in there too—particularly after a few failures in a class. The fast phobia cure can be very useful in such situations.

PART 4

Specific Strategies to Heal "ADHD Dysfunctions"

13

Reorganizing Your Timelines

Do you not see how necessary a world of pains and troubles is to school an intelligence and make it a soul?

JOHN KEATS (1795–1821), BRITISH POET IN A LETTER TO GEORGE AND GEORGIANNA KEATS, APRIL 21, 1819

ONE OF THE MOST COMMON difficulties seen in people who've been identified as having ADHD is that they have a poor sense of past and future. For some, this is so profound that it is largely responsible for their diagnosis as having ADHD. Observing this poor time sense has led some theoreticians to conclude that ADHD must be seated in the frontal lobes of the brain, since it is believed that our sense of time resides there. Some have even gone so far as to propose that ADHD is a specific dysfunction of the frontal lobes, or that this part of the brain is undernourished, underdeveloped, or damaged through some unknown process during childhood. One researcher is even saying that by injecting patients with radioactive substances and then scanning for potentially cancer-causing alpha particles coming out of the radioactive material he injected into their brains, he has determined that much of ADHD is a result of low levels of activity in the frontal lobes.

The biggest problem others have with this type of "research" is that the brain is "plastic." It changes in response to stimuli, and learning actually modifies the flow of blood, levels of metabolism, and apparent levels of neurotransmitters in specific regions of the brain.

For example, research done at Stanford University Medical School by Dr. Lewis Baxter in 1992 found that people with obsessive-compulsive disorder (OCD) display a unique signature in their brain scans, particularly when they're obsessing on something such as wanting to wash their hands a dozen times a day. If you give them Prozac or one of the other drugs used to treat OCD, Dr. Baxter found, their brain scans will become "normalized" while they're on the drug. When this was first discovered, it was hailed by some as proving that OCD was biological, not psychological, and that OCD resided in a particular part of the brain, which could be seen on the scan. By changing the brain's neurochemical environment through the use of drugs that modify levels of serotonin, the pharmacologists said, it was possible to fix the "broken" brain.

Then came along a radical form of psychotherapy called Exposure, Response, and Prevention (ERP) therapy, pioneered by Dr. Victor Meyer. With ERP therapy, a person is exposed to the "trigger" that causes them to start obsessing, but then is physically restrained from acting out their compulsion. They're shown the sink, for example, but held back from it and not allowed to wash their hands. After some time (minutes for some, hours for others), the obsession peters out, and by repeating this process over a period of two to four weeks, most cases of OCD can be—literally—cured. An interesting side effect to ERP therapy is that when a primary obsession is cured, many smaller obsessive behaviors go away as well: there is a permanent change in a person's behavior.

Now comes the really interesting part. When people with OCD are brain-scanned after ERP therapy, their brains are as "normal" as those OCD patients on Prozac. However, they stay that way for the rest of their lives, whereas the people on Prozac lapse back into abnormal scans when the drug is withdrawn.

So what is a brain scan showing: cause or effect? Clearly, this sort of research (which is not unique—this is one example of dozens of studies over the years showing that the brain physically changes as a result of experience or learning new behaviors) argues that when we're looking at a brain scan, in addition to seeing potentially cancer-causing radioactivity, we're also seeing, in many cases, effect and not cause (the obvious exception is when somebody has experienced a stroke or head injury, but that's a whole different topic).

So how can we change our sense of time? Is it possible to learn new ways of experiencing time, so that our brain will change permanently and correct problems such as poor planning, procrastination, and chronic tardiness?

The answer is that we *can* make such changes. And often with surprising ease.

For some people, there is an apparent payoff in being late or disorganized. Psychological theory is filled with examples of people who are always late because it makes them the center of attention or who are disorganized as a way of getting other people to do things for them. This may, however, be another case of mistaking effect for cause. Most such people would tell you in a heartbeat that they'd rather be on time and organized, with regard to their schedule . . . but that they lack the ability to do so.

"Time is a huge, gray vortex for me," one woman said. "Even thinking about tomorrow or next week makes me feel uneasy."

This woman, who'd spent years in psychotherapy and, as a result, seen her sense of time progressively deteriorate, had a good reason to fear looking into the future: that's where her past had come to be, as a result of the "therapy" she'd been undergoing.

Here's how it works. After you read this paragraph, put down this book for a moment and close your eyes. Raise your left and right arms, and with your index fingers point to your past with your left hand and your future with your right hand. Then open your eyes, notice where your hands are pointing, return your arms to normal, and pick the book back up.

Did you do it? If not, do it now.

If you have a pretty well-organized sense of time and are right-handed, you probably pointed up and to the front-right for your future, and down and to the rear-left for your past. One place or another, there *is* a timeline that we all have and that our brain organizes internally as a physical stretch of meta-reality. For some people, though, it resembles a circle or box or tangle of yarn instead of a line.

For example, when I asked the woman mentioned earlier, who dreaded looking at the future, where her future was, she pointed directly in front of her. She saw the future as a series of pictures, one behind the other, straight out in front of her eyes.

This presented her first problem: the near future obscured her view of the far future, since she'd have to look *through* the near-future pictures to see the further-out future. Even worse, when I asked her where her past was, she discovered that parts of it were located in two different places. Much of her past—which she had a very difficult time remembering or finding—was straight out behind her. Of course, if something is behind our head, it's hard to see! But other parts of her past—in particular the traumatic memories of childhood that her therapist had wanted her to repeatedly describe to him in vivid detail over the years—were in front of her, in front even of the pictures of her near future, like tomorrow or the day after.

She had been asked repeatedly by her therapist to, in effect, bring parts of her past out in front and examine them closely. She did so, putting them in front of her future. But the therapist never told her to put the past-pictures back away, and they stayed there out in front, where they haunted her every time she tried to visualize her future in any way. This so frightened her that she stopped planning the future altogether; she couldn't even keep a dentist's appointment.

Another person had his future stretching around to the right in a curve, going back behind him. He could plan a week ahead but couldn't imagine a month ahead because it was behind him, where he couldn't "see" it.

Many people will have their past or future running away from them in a straight line, not slanted up or down. The problem with this is that it becomes impossible to differentiate one time from another: they're either all jumbled together or else only the nearest times are visible and the others are obscured by the near past and near future.

Understanding this, close your eyes again for a moment and notice where your timelines are, then return back to this book.

At a speech I gave on healing ADHD, I asked a room full of about two hundred people to close their eyes and point to their past and future. At least half of the people in the room pointed to places that are not useful for organizing and controlling time, such as directly in front, straight up, behind them, or straight down. When I asked them to then open their eyes and raise their hands if they had difficulty organizing and keeping track of time, the people with the most dysfunctional timeline placements were mostly those who raised their hands acknowledging problems with keeping track of time.

REALIGNING YOUR TIMELINES

There's a simple fix for this problem that comes from NLP. If you do it a few times over a few days, it's permanent, just like the ERP therapy for OCD, and you can do it yourself or walk your child through it.

Here's the technique. Close your eyes, and visualize your timeline again. Then reach out with your real hands as you see imaginary hands in your mind's eye. Grab your past and future timelines, and move them to where they should be, which for most people is up and to the right for the future (about a foot or two to the right of where the arm/hand would stretch in a Nazi salute) and down and to the left for the past (just up and forward a bit from where your hand would be if you were hitchhiking).

Some people feel comfortable with the future on the up-left and the past in the down-right, particularly left-handed people, and that's fine. Others prefer the past and future as a straight line going straight through them: if you do this, it's best that the line go from past-down-left to future-up-right, so that you can always see all parts of it. If you move any part of it behind you, you'll lose some of your easy access to it.

Some people prefer that their past be entirely behind them, and their future totally in front of them. Sometimes this is useful, and you can experiment with it. You can always change your timeline if the way you arrange it doesn't suit you.

Some people find that moving their timeline is easier if a trusted friend or companion guides them through it. If this is the case with you, have that person read this chapter and then walk you through the procedure a few times. If you're one of those people who would rather be on time and organized, this strategy could help you reorient yourself so that you become punctual and methodical.

MOVING PARTS OF THE PAST
BEHIND YOU

Some parts of the past we don't want to have easily available, such as embarrassing moments, painful memories, and events we've already learned from and prefer not to be haunted by. There are several methods to deal with these parts of the past that leave them accessible if they're needed but relocated to a relatively unobtrusive place. Some techniques can also change the charge associated with memories, so we can remember the event but not wince in pain every time we think of it. If you're a Hunter, or your child or someone you know is, it's likely that they have some memories like this, and moving the memories into the past may help the person be better able to stride into the future.

One of the easiest of these techniques is also the oldest that I know of. When I was a child, I remember more than one occasion when one of my parents or some other adult would respond to a complaint of mine, or my tattling on one of my younger brothers, with, "That's behind you now."

It's a phrase most everybody has heard, but few people have wondered, even for a few minutes, where it came from. How can something intangible like a memory or past event be "behind" us?

Perhaps you're familiar with the old custom of throwing salt over the shoulder. There was a time in human history when salt was necessary for survival—it was used as a desiccant and preservative for fish and meats. In many parts of the world, it was more valuable than gold, and wars have been fought over control of salt-rich areas in landlocked Europe and Asia. So the old custom was that if you spilled salt, it was a bad omen, meaning that bad luck would befall you. To ward off the bad luck, you'd take a pinch of salt with the right hand and throw it over the left shoulder.

You can do the same thing when bad memories spill out in front of you. Mentally take them with your right hand and throw them over your left shoulder, into the dark past behind you. If you ever need them again, you can always go back there with a flashlight and look around and find them, but for the moment they're not in the way.

SHATTERING AND CAROUSEL MUSIC

Here are two other NLP methods to dispose of unpleasant and intrusive memories stemming from a life with ADHD. The first is for memories that are mostly in the form of still pictures; the second is for memories that run as movies.

Pictures: Pull up the image of a memory that takes the form of a still picture and you'd just as soon not have around. Put a frame around it, and turn off all the sounds associated with it. Push it back away from you so it's about ten feet away. Paint it on glass so it's fragile and brittle. Turn it to black and white. Now push it far, far away until it's about a foot square, hanging off in the distance. Mentally pick up a stone, and throw it with perfect accuracy at the picture painted on the glass. Watch the glass shatter and the picture dissolve into a million black-and-white pieces, which then dissolve into dust in space.

Movies: Pull up a memory that is complete enough to run as a movie. If it's an associated movie—that is, you see what you would see if you were present in the movie but you don't actually see yourself in the movie—then disassociate it by putting yourself in the movie, so you're watching a movie with yourself in it. Have it start before the memory becomes unpleasant, and run it quickly through, until it goes past its climax and into the time after the event when it was again pleasant. Freeze-frame it there. Now, play the movie backwards, with silly music in the background, such as from a circus calliope or merry-go-round. Make the music as silly as you possibly can. When the movie gets to the beginning, freeze-frame it and turn it to black and white. Repeat the process with the movie black and white. When you're done, most likely, remembering that movie will cause you to smile as you remember how silly the whole thing was.

FLOATING OVER YOUR TIMELINE

Another interesting technique is to float up and over your timeline. As you float backwards over the past, you'll probably see situations where you were hurt or unhappy, possibly as a result of ADHD. The current-day "you" most likely now has resources and knowledge that, if you'd had them at the time, would have prevented you from being wounded by the occurrence you remember. So when you encounter those past "yous," pour into them the resources and strength and knowledge that you now have, so they can resolve and heal their hurts at that time.

Similarly, you may want to float out over your timeline and pour energies and resources and abilities into future yous, which will help make your future work. Both teach and lead your child in learning and mastering these techniques in order to heal the past and activate a successful future.

14

Becoming Multimodally Functional

Heaven lies about us in our infancy!
Shades of the prison-house begin to close
Upon the growing Boy. . . .

WILLIAM WORDSWORTH (1770–1850),
BRITISH POET,"ODE: INTIMATIONS
OF IMMORTALITY FROM RECOLLECTIONS
OF EARLY CHILDHOOD," 1807

MANY PEOPLE MISS MUCH of the experience of life because they're stuck in one primary sensory modality. They see everything around them, but they don't notice the sounds. Or they hear well but miss the physical sensations. Some people live mostly in their feelings and don't see or hear much around them; they're often clumsy and have a great need to touch and be touched. Founder of NLP Richard Bandler reports that he's met a few people whose primary experience of the world is olfactory or gustatory, and more often than not they're obese.

This one-dimensional experience of the world is a form of calcification, an experiential ossification. I call it *attentional ossification*. Over the many years of life, such people come to live more and more in their favorite particular sensory mode, and it then takes a shock to jar them out of it, breaking away some of the rigidity they've built up around their experience of the world. When that happens, they may even feel a bit disoriented, as a person who'd been sitting in a dark room for hours may feel if suddenly the roof were lifted off and it was a bright, sunny day outside.

This can be a particular problem for kids in school. If a child lives primarily in the auditory world, they'll probably be okay, as reading is a form of "talking out loud inside your own head," and when the teacher talks, they can listen. But if they primarily attend to kinesthetic (feeling) or visual channels of sensory input and don't quickly or easily process auditory information, they'll appear to have a problem paying attention. They may even be labeled as having an attentional problem, such as ADHD.

Attentional ossification can extend to all parts of a person's life. People who are severely attentionally ossified will find that most of their memories are single sense only. They remember the visual scene but not the sounds or the feelings. Or they remember the feelings but can't pull up the sights or sound. They may remember the sound of a time past but can't easily access the picture or feelings. If you find that many of your memories are lacking in one or more of the three primary sensory channels, then you may want to do something about your attentional ossification.

INTERACTIVE SENSORY FLEXIBILITY

People with attentional ossification often reveal their "stuckness" by how they talk. People who are stuck in the visual use almost exclusively visual predicates, saying things like, "I'll see you later," or "That's clear to me." Those who are auditory will say, "Talk to you later," or "Good hearing from you," or "Yeah, I know what you're talking about." Kinesthetic people will say, "Stay in touch," or "I have a good feeling about that," or "You build a strong case for that."

As an exercise, for the next twenty-four hours, start noticing the predicates people use when they speak and what those words say about how they experience the world. You'll find it fascinating, and it'll give you insights into other people that will help you establish better rapport and communication with them (we'll discuss that in chapter 18).

NLP also advocates playing with your sensory systems when interacting with other people. Rather than using your own preferred fallback phrasing, using novel phrasing will keep your brain stimulated as you consider your response more intentionally, which will help center you in the situation and present moment. If you usually use visual predicates (the most common), instead try using auditory or kinesthetic ones. Or experiment with mixing predicates in a sentence. So instead of saying, "Yes, I see that using the Johnson widget would give us a clear advantage as we fine-tune our future manufacturing plans," you may want to try, "Yes, I have a strong sense that the Johnson widget will propel us forward, particularly as we mull over and discuss our future manufacturing plans." It's fun and, as you'll find in a few pages, can be a very useful skill to have.

Everybody is attentionally ossified to some smaller or greater extent. We all have preferred systems that we use to experience and represent the world. These representational systems tend to stay with us for a lifetime, although a well-balanced person will find that they can move from one to another without difficulty and that most memories have a variety of senses in them.

EXPANDING YOUR ATTENTIONAL FREEDOM

There's a simple exercise, which I first learned several decades ago as part of a training program in meditation, that works quite well to help break up and clean away attentional calcium. The result of doing this exercise daily for a few weeks has led to, for me and many of the people I've shared it with, a richer, deeper, and more soulful experience of life itself.

Twenty or more years ago, I spoke at a conference on EEG Neurofeedback in Key West. Psychologist Les Fehmi shared a variation of this exercise with us, which is also from NLP, saying that by teaching it to children with ADHD, he was able to reduce the severity of their ADHD symptoms. He also noted that when they hooked up an electroencephalograph (or EEG—a device that passively reads the electrical activity generated by the brain) to the kids' brains, he and his research team noticed that whenever the kids shifted from one sensory state to another, there was a spike in alpha-wave brain wave activity. Alpha waves were quite the craze back in the 1960s, as they were thought to be the wave patterns associated with blissful or meditative states. While it's apparently not quite that simple, we do know that alpha waves play an important role in having a healthy mind and the ability to experience "peak" states. The times of the day when you are experiencing the greatest intensity of alpha waves are just as you drift off to sleep at night and just as you awaken, in the seconds before you open your eyes in the morning.

I've used the following exercise for years in situations where I'd otherwise get bored and have suggested this with good effect to a number of ADHD kids. If I'm sitting in a boring meeting, I'll just start state shifting. Notice what I'm seeing, then what I'm hearing, then what I'm feeling, and so forth. Sometimes I'll just do it with one or two or three senses: it doesn't take much to bring about a deep feeling of calm and a reconnection with the life of the moment.

So here's the exercise. You'll want to read it through a few times until it's all clear to you, and then do it in one complete pass.

- **See:** Sit in a comfortable position, and notice what you're seeing in front of you. Notice its color, size, clarity, brightness, texture— all the visual details.

- **Hear:** Now, while still looking at what's in front of you, let the sounds in the room, or even the lack of sounds, become the most interesting thing in your world. The sight is still there, but notice the sounds.

- **Feel:** After ten seconds or so of that, allow your attention to shift to how you feel. Notice the sensations of your body: the feeling of your clothes on your skin, the breath moving through your windpipes, and your butt against the seat. Go through your body from head to toe and notice all the different feelings there.

- **Smell and Taste:** Now, notice the smells in the room and any tastes you may have in your mouth. Notice how different parts of your tongue sense different tastes.

- **Observe Time:** Notice your sensation of the passage of time. It's as if you're standing in the river of time, and it's flowing past you. The past is always out there, the future is always out there, but you are always *here,* completely in the *now.* This *now* is the only time that you've ever experienced; it's the only time there is. The past is gone, and the future doesn't yet exist. It never will, in fact: when its time comes, it'll be the *now.* Notice your presence in the room *now.*

- **Sense Space:** Inside your skull are two sensory organs whose job is to detect gravity and help you orient yourself relative to it. This is, literally, an often-overlooked sixth sense, sometimes referred to as the vestibular system. Notice your orientation to the rest of the room. Sense the empty spaces between you and the things around you. Like fish who don't notice the water they swim in, we usually don't notice the empty spaces all around us. Notice them.

- **Examine Thinking:** Thinking is a mechanical activity of the mammalian brain. It usually runs on autopilot, chattering away like a drunken monkey. Notice how your mind generates thinking. It's that thinking that pulls you away from experiencing *now* more often. Interesting, eh? Put your thinking into a head-sized ball and visualize it in front of you. Look at it, listen to it, and feel it. Now, put it back in your head.

- *Witness Self-ness:* There is, within you, a place where your sense of who you *really* are is located. Most people visualize it in their heart. All your opinions, fears, dreams, ambitions, likes, dislikes, guilts, hopes—this is the stuff that makes up *you*. Move that out from your body for a few moments and notice it, love it, feel compassion for it. Then return it within you.

Now, cycle through them again, or at least the first four. The entire process should only take a few minutes, and you can do it virtually anytime, anywhere (though because it can tend to be profoundly relaxing, it's probably not a good idea to do this when driving or operating heavy machinery).

It's a good idea to make this exercise a daily part of your life for a few weeks. You may want to attach it to something else, like getting up in the morning. Do it after you wake up, but before you climb out from under the covers. Or if you do daily meditation practice, use it to open your practice: it'll have a significant and positive effect on the quality of your meditation. If you say prayers daily, you may want to do it before your prayers, as it's a great way to put yourself in contact with the reality of life and divinity all around you all the time. It's also a great strategy to use when you feel the urge to reconnect with the sensation of being alive.

15

Building New Motivation Strategies

Let it be your constant method to look into the design of people's actions, and see what they would be at, as often as it is practicable; and to make this custom the more significant, practice it first upon yourself.

SMALLCAPS MARCUS AURELIUS (121–180),
ROMAN EMPEROR, *MEDITATIONS*

WHILE I WAS IN ENGLAND traveling around and giving speeches about ADD, in one city I visited with a family with a teenage son who'd been put on an antipsychotic medication for his ADD. (This practice is quite common in the United Kingdom; apparently, the doctors get less hassle from parents and the authorities when using these "zombie" drugs than they get with Ritalin, and the kids become quite docile, which seems to please the teachers.) The young man had been in trouble with the police, thrown out of school, in several fistfights with other kids that left him or them with scars, and was generally viewed by his family as an inconvenience and embarrassment.

"Richard has ADD: he is completely unmotivated," his mother complained over dinner. "He doesn't want to do a damn thing."

I looked at Richard, who was poking his potatoes with his fork as if he expected they may explode. "Is that true, Richard?" I said.

He glanced up at me, then back at the potatoes. "Yeah."

"He hates school and won't help out around the house," his mother interjected before I could speak. "He has a terrible attitude and has kicked in two of our doors because of his rages. But his biggest problem is that he's unmotivated."

"You have no motivation, Richard?" I said.

He took a bite of the potatoes. "Nope. None."

This intrigued me, because it's simply impossible. "What about drinking beer?" I said, having heard of his drunken exploits.

He brightened. "Yeah, I like that."

"Walking around in town? Hanging out with your friends?"

"Yeah, that's OK."

"Driving fast."

"I'm good at that," he said and laughed.

"Skateboarding?"

"Yeah, for sure."

"Do you do all those things?"

He nodded, chewing his food. "Uh huh."

"Frequently?"

"Yeah. All the time."

"You get out of bed, get dressed, and go out and do them?"

"Sure. I'd look pretty silly if I was naked, wouldn't I?"

I turned to his mother and said, "He doesn't seem unmotivated to me."

She looked positively shocked. "But he won't do his schoolwork! He won't help around the house! He won't get a job!"

"I agree that he's not motivated in those areas," I said. "But he certainly is motivated to do the things *he* wants to do."

Lest it seem that I was playing semantic games over dinner, let me note here that this is a very important distinction. The only truly "unmotivated" people I've ever come across have been either clinically depressed, comatose, or dead. Everybody else is busily in the process of doing or getting *something* they want, even if it's just another bowl of ice cream and the TV remote control.

The question, then, is not, "How to get motivated?" but instead, "How to shift our motivation from things that are not useful, or time wasters, and connect them to things that are useful and will help us accomplish our life goals?"

MOVING TOWARD OR MOVING FROM

Motivation strategies fall into two basic categories. Virtually everybody is either in the process of moving toward something pleasurable or moving away from something painful. While this may sound (if you're auditory, "seem" if you're primarily visual, or "feel" if you're kinesthetic) like a restatement of B. F. Skinner's core hypothesis, or even Pavlov's early work, it's really rather more profound in that it's more simple.

No matter what you're doing, or when you're doing it, you're doing it for one of two reasons: to get pleasure or avoid pain. This is even true—perhaps *especially* true—of altruistic behavior, which moves us toward the pleasure of knowing we've done something good.

One person may go to work to get the pleasure of the paycheck or the pleasure of the social interaction. Another may go to avoid the pain of unemployment.

The way to determine which is their primary motivational strategy is to ask them what they visualize when they wake up in the morning and think about going to work. Is it the paycheck and the friends? Or the unemployment line and future job search if they don't make it in on time?

Both moving toward pleasure and avoiding pain are positive goals. Both work to the benefit of the human organism. And both have their appropriate places: if you encounter a rattlesnake in the forest, the motivation of getting back to the cabin with a hot cup of coffee may not make you move anywhere near as quickly as the thought of dying an agonizing death from rattlesnake venom.

Moving toward pleasure strategies are usually best for long-term goals. They have staying power. They make us feel good. We enjoy waking up in the morning if we know that our day is going to be devoted to moving toward pleasure. We enjoy going to sleep knowing that the next day we'll again be pursuing pleasure. Pleasure is, well, *pleasurable.*

Avoiding pain, on the other hand, is an even more immediately powerful motivation strategy. It was wired into us by nature—as it is in all animals—and it gives us access to the most raw, bright, and loud neurochemicals in our bodies. The adrenaline compounds that are associated with the avoiding-pain systems are capable of making your heart race so hard and fast it can literally burst. They can freeze your digestive system, paralyze your muscles, or stimulate you to feats of strength and endurance that would have otherwise been completely impossible. While the avoiding-pain systems don't have the staying power of the seeking-pleasure ones, they make up for that in raw power.

The problem for most people, though, is that in many cases, they connect the wrong strategy to their goals.

Because the avoiding-pain system is so powerful, it's taught to children from a young age. Parents use threats to keep kids in line, get them to do what the parents want, and keep them from doing what the parents don't want. The threats work, at least for a short while, because the kids are interested in avoiding pain. They don't want that spanking, or to have to sit in their room for an hour, or to be publicly humiliated.

Repeated exposure to this strategy can have negative consequences for later life. As a person grows up, they're very familiar with the avoiding-pain mechanism, so they call on it internally when they need a short-term jolt. The kid at college wakes up and imagines getting thrown out of school for flunking out, losing the funding of their scholarship or parents, and having to look for a job delivering pizza. It's a painful enough scenario that they hop out of bed and begin to dress for class.

After a few weeks, the pictures don't instill the adrenaline rush anymore. As with most negative stimuli, the student becomes progressively less and less frightened. So they have to make progressively worse pictures to propel them out of bed in the morning: living under a highway overpass, being disowned by family, contracting a fatal disease from lack of sanitation and medical care.

This daily immersion in progressively more traumatic negative images takes its toll. Soon the student dreads school: it reminds them of all the negative things they're trying to avoid. They hate getting up in the morning. Even the bed itself is becoming associated with these negative feelings, and they start to drink at night to get to sleep. A full-force downward spiral is underway.

While a negative strategy may be useful from time to time on a college campus—for example, to get out of the way of an oncoming bus—applying it to daily life is a great way to make life miserable. And the same is true of just about anyplace else, from the home to the workplace.

On the other hand, our hypothetical student may come up with a positive motivation strategy to get up every morning. They could visualize their parents hugging them and telling them how proud they are of their grades and academic achievements or picture the envious looks of siblings. They could hear the sound of people congratulating them as they use newfound knowledge to unlock the secrets of life and win the Nobel Prize. They may see themselves relaxing next to the pool in the backyard of the spiffy new house bought with the high salary earned as a result of their having completed a college education and a Ph.D. If any of these pictures become stale, they can simply replace them with better and brighter ones: there's no negative fallout from setting progressively higher and happier goals for yourself. And with this moving-toward-pleasure motivation strategy, they look forward to waking up every morning, getting out of bed and off to class, and coming back to their dorm room so they can get a good night's sleep to begin the next day afresh.

We all know people who primarily use avoiding pain strategies in their lives. They complain about things as a way of life, since making things negative is motivational to them. They seem to revel in their negativity and fatalism, and from the outside it looks as if it must be a real chore for them. In fact, it is.

We also know people who use moving toward pleasure as their primary internal motivational system. They're bright and cheerful, and always looking at the positive side of things and trying to see the best in just about everything. From the outside, it looks as if they're enjoying life most of the time. In fact, they are.

The rub is that few people realize that they're even using a motivational strategy—with just about everything they do, every moment of every day—and even fewer realize that they can change their strategies just as quickly as they can change the way they wear their hair.

But you know it now, and if you go through this process with your child, they do too.

Begin to examine your strategies and the stories you tell yourself about how things will be either when you get what you want or don't do what you need to do. Ask yourself if you're using negative or positive strategies, avoiding pain or seeking pleasure. Where you find the negative strategies, visualize what life could be like if you replaced them with positive, moving-toward-pleasure strategies.

Keep in mind that you can always use avoiding-pain strategies whenever you need to. But you can choose! One of the central tenets of this work is that we never want to do away with a resource; instead, we want to add new ones. Every behavior is potentially useful, even seemingly dysfunctional things such as bedwetting or getting into fights. The key is having the personal power to choose when to use a particular resource, rather than doing things without conscious direction.

To replace an avoiding-pain strategy with a going-toward-pleasure strategy is really quite simple. Visualize and write down all the good, pleasant, happy things that can come from your doing whatever it is you need to feel motivated to accomplish. Work with the submodalities associated with the images—changing their contrast, brightness, sounds, and so on—until you fine-tune them to peak intensity. Then practice bringing them up and holding them out in front of you as a motivation to go forward.

TALKING YOURSELF OUT OF PROCRASTINATION

Procrastination is a characteristic that's often identified in pop psychology as a hallmark of attention deficit hyperactive disorder. People with ADHD have a lousy sense of time, some will say. They can't concentrate long enough to follow through, others say. And some say that folks with ADHD are so poorly inhibited that they can't clamp down on their mind long enough to finish the task at hand. The Freudians say that people procrastinate because they fear success, whereas others say procrastinators put things off because they fear failure.

All of these may have some truth, but there's another option that I've found to be true for many people who have procrastination as a problem. *People who procrastinate have an obnoxious and painful internal voice yelling at them.*

The internal motivation strategy for most procrastinators I've known is to have an internal voice from one of their parts, which says, in a loud, aggressive, and often obnoxious tone: "You'd better do this now or there will be dire consequences!"

What a great voice to ignore! This type of motivation, right out of a novel by Dickens, is certainly not a voice that most people would want to listen to. And they don't.

Imagine something that you think you should do, and try out such an internal voice telling you to do it. How does it feel? Odds are it's unpleasant, and perhaps you even have another internal voice saying, "Hey, buddy, jump off a cliff!"

Insomniacs* often have a similar problem. For years I noticed that when I had a lot on my mind, I also had trouble sleeping. I'd toss and turn, trying to push away the intruding thoughts, sometimes even writing things down on a pad in an attempt to get rid of the obnoxious intruders. But none of it worked: there was still that internal self-talk about how important/worrisome/disastrous the issue at hand was. Then I heard Richard Bandler speak at an NLP training, and in a seemingly offhand manner, he pointed out that most insomniacs have "lousy internal tonality." They talk to themselves in shrill, whiny, nasal, urgent, worried voices, he said (among other things). The solution he suggested was to simply change the voice!

I tried it that night. When I heard my internal voice ranting on, I slowed it down, made it soft and somewhat sexy, and then turned it to a nurturing voice. Ahhhhhh . . . within ten minutes, I was asleep.

For procrastinators the problem is often the same. They have a hugely irritating internal voice ranting at them about what they should do, and it becomes a badge of honor to ignore or resist that obnoxious voice.

So here's a quick way to overcome procrastination that you can do yourself and teach your children.

---

*As documented in *ADHD: A Hunter in a Farmer's World*, people diagnosed with ADHD are far more likely to struggle with sleep.

Imagine something you need to do in the near future. Now, imagine a curious, soft, nurturing, sexy voice *inviting* you to accomplish the task and pointing out to you all of the warm, wonderful, pleasant things that will result from your action. If the old, obnoxious voice is still there, grab it with a loving hand and adjust its tone, pace, and volume to be sexy, curious, soft, and nurturing (or whatever other adjectives work best for you). The *very same words* said in a different tonality will have dramatically different results.

16

Anchoring Positive States for Future Access

If we are always arriving and departing, it is also true that we are eternally anchored. One's destination is never a place but rather a new way of looking at things.

HENRY MILLER (1891–1980), AMERICAN WRITER,
*BIG SUR AND THE ORANGES OF
HIERONYMUS BOSCH*, 1957

FOR YEARS I HAULED AROUND a black leather chair from business to business. I bought it at an auction back in the early 1970s when I opened one of my first companies, and every time I sold one business and started another that chair went with me. Whenever I sat in it, I got an immediate feeling of competence, capability, and enthusiasm. I once had another chair—a rocking chair—that was associated for me with feelings of tranquility and meditation: I'd used it to meditate in for years.

When I first learned meditation in the 1960s, in fact, I was told to always meditate in the same place, sitting on the same chair or cushion. "That way your sitting area will become invested with spiritual vibrations, which you can feel whenever you go there and sit down to meditation," my meditation teacher said. He was right.

I also remember my grandma's antique store in northern Michigan. My grandfather had a cabinet-making shop in the back, and the front of the store was piled so high (in my childhood memory) with antiques, knickknacks, and bric-a-brac that you could hardly navigate through the narrow aisles. The place smelled musty—of old wood and wax and books. Today, whenever I walk into an antique store or Salvation Army store, the smell brings back a flood of pleasant memories of my childhood.

These sensory inputs—the feeling of the chair, the appearance of the meditation area, the smell of Grandma's store—are called *anchors*. They're deeply associated in my brain with old feelings, and when I encounter them the feelings rush back. You have them too: anchors are part of everybody's life.

The concept of anchors was first discovered by Pavlov, who found that he could cause dogs to anchor the sound of a bell to a sensation of hunger. For some weeks he rang a bell each time before he fed his dogs. Eventually, the bell became such a deeply seated anchor that simply ringing it would cause the dogs to salivate.

When you think about it, that's really a pretty radical thing. The dogs' internal neurochemistry—millions of chemical reactions, levels of various hormones and digestive juices, and their level of blood salinity and saliva production—all changed in a few seconds. And that change was in response to a *sound* that, in and of itself, had nothing whatever to do with food.

Anchors can, of course, be negative or positive. Some people had such a painful experience of school, for example, that even going to a school play for their child or a meeting with their child's teachers in a classroom after hours evokes a sense of dread. Others enjoyed the circus or carnival so much as children that they become age-regressed and gleeful when they visit such places as adults.

We create and respond to anchors constantly. Many have to do with place—sitting at our desk, our dinner table, and on our bed all bring up different emotional states. Some are associated with smells—the smell of a library or grandma's house. Others have to do with what we hear—a particular song that evokes memories and emotions or a tone of voice that makes us reactive.

The strength of an anchor depends on how intense its first impression was and how many times it was revisited after that. All the anchors I mentioned above derived their strength from having been repeated over and over, a process that is often referred to as *stacking anchors*. On the other hand, I was once in a near-crash in a commercial jet, and it took quite a while for me to not feel a sense of dread and terror whenever I walked onto a plane. That anchor was installed in less than ten seconds, but the installation went very deep because of the strength of the emotions I experienced when we all thought we were going to die.

REMOVING ANCHORS

Several of the methods discussed earlier to change the charge associated with negative memories can also be applied to negative anchors. In particular, the NLP fast phobia cure method works quite well for this.

It's also possible to create or remove anchors associated with aspects of "ADHD-ness" as part of an overall strategy of personal behavior modification. Consider the things you'd like to do more of or do better, and consider ways to positively anchor them; consider the things you'd like to discard and start associating them with negative anchors, or remove the positive anchors that are holding them to you.

Another way to remove old anchors is to reassociate them with something else. After my frightening experience on the plane, I always carried with me onto a plane a book that I really wanted to read. Enjoying reading is a more powerful anchor for me than being afraid of flying, and after a few flights with a good book, I was able to relax on a plane . . . so long as I had something interesting to read. Adding a glass of wine to the flight—another positive and pleasant anchor for me—caused me to flip in a few months (OK, about a year) from dreading flying to not particularly liking it to looking forward to it. The anchor of the plane had shifted from an association with dying to an association with escapist reading and feeling a warm glow from a glass of wine.

INSTALLING ANCHORS

Anchors can be quickly installed, even in highly artificial situations. For example, have somebody sit in front of you, and ask them to close their eyes and remember a time when they felt really, really, really good. Just as their smile reaches maximum intensity, squeeze their knee. Have them repeat the exercise, and do the same thing, stacking that knee-squeeze anchor three or four times. Then ask them to just sit with their mind blank and think of nothing particularly important. While they're in that place, fire off the anchor by squeezing their knee: you'll see an immediate smile.

For most of us, simple postural changes produce a similar result from a lifetime of associating them with a particular feeling. Sitting or standing up straight, breathing deeply, putting a smile on your face, and similar things are memorialized in songs and clichés because they're so universally known (such as the song "Put On a Happy Face").

Because we lay down anchors constantly, which reaffect us when fired off again, it's important that we be intentional about our anchors. For example, there are thousands of anchors you've connected with your home and place of work. What's the feeling you get when you're called into the boss's office? At lunch with others? At the place where you do most of your work? In the car when you're driving to or from work? When the phone rings? For each of us, these anchors will have different meanings. Some people love the boss's office, while others dread it. And on and on.

To a large extent, our motivation strategies affect our workplace anchors. Negative motivators (avoiding pain) become progressively more and more negative about their place of work; often they'll change jobs "just to escape the pain," which they've largely inflicted on themselves by repeatedly bringing up negative motivating images to kick-start themselves at work.

Positive motivators (moving toward pleasure) are continually anchoring their workplace as well, but they're creating progressively more positive and happy anchors. Such people often spend twenty years or more at the same job and miss it when they retire.

Because the workplace is a minefield of anchors, one useful policy for management is to always have one room for "positive and motivational" meetings to be held in and another, separate room for "difficult or punishing" meetings. If the same conference room or office is used for both, it'll become so anchor-confused that highly unpredictable results may come from the meetings you hold there. Teachers can also consider the ways they structure space within the classroom. It may be helpful for them to position themselves in certain places for particular tasks, from praising to criticizing to lighter or deeper dives into subject matter. The key is to remember the place where you stand (and, often, the posture associated with it) for the anchors to be successful.

This proves the wisdom of the old motherly advice to newlyweds to "never go to bed angry." If you fight with your spouse in your bed, the bed itself becomes an anchor for negative feelings. Repeat that a few times and the negative feelings may become so intense that it's difficult to recapture the original feelings of lust and love and even sleepiness with which a marital bed is normally associated. Instead, define a place in the house, or outside the house, which is where you'll go to fight, and only use it for that purpose. Don't fight in the kitchen or living room or car: those places will become anchored to that state. Use the garage, the basement, or some other place that's only there for that purpose.

You can also create anchors for other people. Use a particular tone of voice, set of words, posture, touch, or facial gesture whenever they do the behavior you want to anchor or whenever you do the behavior you want them anchored to. Occasionally fire off the anchors to test them. Now they're there for when you need them.

PROCESSING NEGATIVES

In order for a thought or emotion to be anchored, it must first be in consciousness. Oddly enough, one of the best ways to bring something to consciousness is to tell somebody *not* to think about it. This is particularly problematic when parents tell their kids things like "Don't run into the traffic," which *requires* the child to imagine running into traffic to understand.

For example, for a moment, don't think about circus elephants rampaging down the middle of the street in front of your home. Don't think about them at all.

Or don't think about the fact that in the twenty-four hours since this time yesterday, fifty-four thousand people on this planet have died of starvation. Don't even imagine that each and every one of them died as an individual person and that thirty-eight thousand of them were children.

It's impossible to perform a mental negative. If I say *not* to think about pink flamingos, first your brain must bring up an image of them so that it'll know what *not* to think about.

Even more interesting—although probably beyond the scope of this book—is the old Ericksonian hypnotic technique of concatenating negatives. If none of your sentences never contain not even three or four negative commands—or at least not not-positive ones—then the result is that the listener's conscious mind goes "tilt" and turns off its discriminating function for a few moments because it can't keep track of all those negatives.

During that time, you can deliver powerful hypnotic commands, which bypass the conscious mind and go directly into the unconscious. For example, consider that there was a time when you didn't know anything, but you didn't know what you didn't know, because you were not all that conscious about what you could know and what you couldn't know. Soon after that, as you became a bit older, you discovered that there were lots of things you didn't know, but you didn't know what they were, other than *that* they were, so you didn't know what you didn't know, but you also knew that there were things you didn't know, even though you didn't know what they were. Then you became a teenager, and for a brief while there was nothing you didn't know. And now you probably don't know at all what you don't know, don't know what you missed knowing, and don't know what you don't want to know, because then, of course, you'd have to know it first to not-know it, and you don't want to know that, do you? Maybe and maybe not.

Out of confusion comes clarity. Every single time you have learned something new in your entire life, it was at first confusing. But then you learned it, and it became clear, strong, understandable. You can do that now with the material in this book.

17

Acquiring New Learning Skills

To look backward for a while is to refresh the eye, to restore it, and to render it the more fit for its prime function of looking forward.

Margaret Fairless Barber (1869–1901),
British writer, *The Roadmender*, 1902

Whether you are ADHD or not, one of the easiest ways to learn something is to learn it backwards.

Over the years, a number of NLP practitioners reported that their "learning-disabled" clients, children and adults alike, had difficulty making stable, clear imaginary pictures. Somehow, for some reason that nobody knows but more than a few suspect has to do with watching television, these people have either lost, or never developed in the first place, the ability to create pictures in their heads.

The visual cortex, that part of the occipital portion of the brain that processes images, is absolutely huge when compared to just about any other single-function part of the brain. It's ten to fifty times larger (depending on how narrowly you define it), for example, than the temporal-region auditory processing areas such as Wernicke's or Broca's areas. It's huge.

The reason for this is pretty obvious, when you think of it. In one microsecond-long picture—what you see right now when you look up quickly from this book and then back—there are literally billions of individual elements that go into making up that image. For the brain to process this, for us to be able to discriminate between over a million different colors and remember these images for years at a time, it takes enormous brain processing horsepower.

For this reason, the visual part of the brain is one of the most powerful tools you have available in your mental toolkit. And it's why if you can see something, or make a picture of it, you'll remember it long, long, long after the rote memory (trying to remember the words) part has gone.

Unfortunately, this simple fact about how we learn hasn't yet made a complete transit from the laboratory to the classroom. Teachers still ask kids to recite things over and over, making them cram them into those tiny auditory-processing parts of the brain in order to memorize them. Very little emphasis is put on making pictures, except perhaps by the occasional highly visual teacher.

So to learn something, make a picture of it.

Imagine yourself sitting in a classroom, and over your head is one of those thought balloons like in the comic strips. And in that thought balloon is a picture of you drawing a picture on an easel. If you can make that picture, one of the strongest memories you'll carry away from this book is that you can learn things when you make a picture of them.

But as mentioned earlier, many "learning-disabled" people—those with "deficits" and "disorders"—have a difficult time making pictures. Their imagination apparatus has become sluggish.

Fortunately, the solution is easy and painless. As with learning to ride a bike or drive a car or read or type or anything else, there is one main thing that will quickly produce proficiency at making mental pictures: practice.

But how does a person know when they're making good mental pictures? This is where the "backwards" part comes in.

Try this experiment. Find somebody—child or adult—who thinks of themselves as a poor speller. Get a few vocabulary words that they don't know how to spell and would like to learn. Let's say that one of those words is, for example, *Connecticut*. Or for the younger set, perhaps *llama*.

Now, have them make a mental picture of a llama or the map of the state of Connecticut. When they say they have the picture, ask them to use a mental paintbrush to paint the word on the picture, one letter at a time, saying the letters out loud as they do it.

Now comes the reality test. If they're really a "disabled" poor speller, odds are that they made a fuzzy, jiggling, poorly defined picture and therefore can't easily pull it back up and read the word off it. So ask them to look at the picture and read the word off it *backwards*. In order to do this, they *must* stabilize their picture. And that exercise of stabilizing the picture, done just a few times (sometimes it takes as many as twenty or thirty repetitions, each time with a different word), teaches them how to make clear, stable, useful pictures.

Memory teacher Harry Lorayne* takes this a step further. If you can make a picture, he says, and make it an *absurd* picture, then you'll have instantly committed something to memory. This method, which Aristotle first taught as a way of memorizing speeches (he called it the *loci* method, since he used absurd objects mentally placed in his house as speech-item reminders), has been around for a long time. It's the basis of techniques to remember people's names: think of Loraine having rain pouring out of her hair and over her face or Bill covered with dollar bills (see how hard it is not to imagine things?). If you need to remember a to-do list, just make each item absurd and then link them together. The store is exploding, with loaves of bread

---

The Memory Book by Harry Lorayne and Jerry Lucas

popping out of the windows. They rain down on the bank down the street. This is causing money to flow out the front door of the bank like a river, right into the front door of the dry-cleaner's shop. Pick up the bread; cash the check; pick up the clothes. The list could as easily be twenty items as three.

When NLP practitioners began teaching kids how to dissolve their spelling disability by reading off pictures backwards and practicing making absurd images, many noticed an interesting side effect: the kids became more proficient learners in practically every area of academics. They became better and faster learners of life skills. They could follow directions. They didn't lose things as often.

They had learned how to learn.

You can too, and you can teach your children. Now.

18

Learning New Communication Skills

We're born alone, we live alone, we die alone. Only through our love and friendship can we create the illusion for the moment that we're not alone.

ORSON WELLES (1915–1985), AMERICAN ACTOR,
DIRECTOR, WRITER, *SOMEONE TO LOVE*, 1987
(RELEASED AFTER HIS DEATH)

GOOD COMMUNICATORS KNOW a few things that incompetent communicators don't. The primary three are *pacing, matching,* and *building rapport.* Very often, people with ADHD have been spending so much time just trying to keep up with the world or struggling with schools and jobs that don't suit their temperament that they've failed to learn these lessons of good communication. But they're easy to learn and don't take a lot of practice to become second nature.

Natural communicators—people who are intuitively good at conveying their ideas and thoughts to others—usually do these things by instinct, whether in person, on the phone, or even in writing. Nobody told them to, but somewhere along the way they picked up the skills. Odds are they had an early role model—a teacher or parent or older sibling—who was a master communicator and they simply modeled that person, picking up the techniques by practicing them without knowing that there were words or names for any of them. Perhaps they modeled a remote person they didn't even know personally, such as a writer or TV personality. However they did it, they became good at communicating, and the more they did it the better they got.

The concept of breaking these skills out and naming them is just from the last century, although, again, the ancient Greeks had more than a few words to say on the overall concepts. Numerous people over the years, and in particular Richard Bandler and John Grinder, observed highly effective communicators in a number of different settings and then asked, "What is it that they're all doing in common that makes them so effective?" From this questioning process came the core concepts of pacing, matching, and building rapport.

When you master these skills, you can be comfortable and effective in virtually any social or business situation, from talking one-on-one to giving a speech for a room full of people. You'll find that others have a better understanding of what it is you're trying to communicate, and—perhaps most interestingly—you'll discover that you have a clearer and more solid grasp of what they're trying to say.

PACING AND MATCHING

Here's a tip for ADHDers who have trouble communicating or getting their way when it's important. I remember I was stuck in the Salt Lake City airport because of a huge snowstorm that had started in the Midwest and then swept all the way down to Atlanta. I'd been waiting at the airport for a flight out for most of the day, and I wasn't alone in my situation: the airport was crowded with people whose flights, like mine, had been delayed, rerouted, or outright canceled. The snowstorm was echoing through the entire air traffic system, having already shut down several cities.

Sitting in my airline's frequent flyer lounge, I took a glass of wine and a book to a seat near the reservations desk, where I could keep my eye out for possible changes in flights. From the desk I could hear a man progressively raising his voice.

"When can you get me out of here? I have business to do! This is a disaster for me!" A man with a red face wearing a dark pinstripe suit was leaning over the counter, speaking rapidly with short, clipped words and a faint New York accent.

"Well, sir, you see we don't have any control here. . ." said the man behind the desk, sitting at a computer, his voice slow and soft with a thick southern drawl.

The New Yorker interrupted him. "I don't care what you can't do! Tell me what you can do! I know you can find a plane to put me on. You just don't want to pay another airline to fly me!"

"No, sir," the agent said, his voice soft and deliberate. "The situation is that none of the airlines have capacity right now . . ."

"Get somebody to bump somebody!" the man barked.

And on it went for a few minutes, until the New Yorker stomped away angrily, leaving the reservations agent shaking his head at the man's bad manners.

I made a mental note. Ten minutes or so later, I walked over to the reservations agent and, speaking at the same speed I'd heard him talk with earlier, asked him how it looked for my flights. He brightened right up and energetically began searching for new flight options for me.

I wish I could say that my having paced the man's speaking speed got me the flight I wanted, but it didn't. The point, though, was that he felt that I *understood* him, that I was on his wavelength. I found myself relaxing into his cadence of speech, and it made me feel closer to him too. We understood each other. Sympatico. Brothers in slow speech.

If I'd had to talk with the New Yorker, I would have sped up my speech to match his. Sometimes, I even find myself picking up people's accents without realizing I'm doing it. Years ago, when I first discovered myself doing it, it seemed odd. Now it's just there.

I remember being in a meeting with one of the larger clients for an advertising agency I used to own in Atlanta. There were eight or ten people in the room, and I was answering questions about a job we were working on, as well as offering suggestions on their marketing plans. I'd discovered that this committee in this company had their own pace, which largely followed the natural pace of the VP who ran the meeting. Everybody pretty much followed his pace, except one woman who, because of her slow and deliberate style, irritated everybody as she raised her voice to finish her long-winded (to them) sentences. The room had a pace. Those who didn't keep up with it fell to the side.

Pacing isn't just about speed.* Notice how your voice changes when you speak with different people. I find that my voice changes as much as an octave between different people, depending in some part on how they're speaking. Try pacing and matching their speed, tone of voice, and use of language (slang, regionalisms, use of obscenity, and so on.).

Pacing is also about the type of speech used, the predicates and other words. Is the person using simple sentences and short words or complex sentences and polysyllabic words? Are they talking primarily in visual metaphors or auditory ones or kinesthetic ones?

This last point of predicates is a crucial one. If the other person is

---

*There are also issues of command that have to do with voice. Just like someone who extends a hand to shake with their palm down is signifying their intent to dominate and a person who extends a hand with the palm up shows their willingness to be dominated, voice tone can convey relative power positions. Generally, the lower the tone of voice is in comparison to others, the more power a person is claiming for themselves.

describing their experience using visual predicates, for example, and you use auditory or kinesthetic ones, you not only run the risk of not communicating, but you may even cause them to feel irritated with you (although they would probably never be able to say why). I've seen this happen in many situations over the years, and it's particularly critical in intimate or highly personal communications. A therapist who responds to a client's saying, "I just feel like the world is crushing me. Life is so rough," with a statement such as, "Well, let's see if we can get a better focus on that—what do you see as the main problem?" is doomed. If, on the other hand, the therapist were to match the person's predicates (e.g., "Let's try to get a handle on that situation. What do you find is your biggest source of pain?"), there's a very good chance that positive and productive change could take place. When you match people's predicates, they believe that you understand their representation of reality, as if you can read their minds or have had similar experiences as they have. When you're not synchronous with their predicates, they get the feeling that you don't understand them or their world.

Pacing and matching also have to do with body posture, rate of breathing, and gestures. Sit in a room full of people, pick one person you don't know in the room, and imitate their body posture. You'll notice shortly that your target person will react, either changing their body posture away from you and your posture or else moving toward you in some way, getting physically closer or pointing their body toward you. If you copy them too closely, they may become irritated; if it's too far off, they won't notice it. In any case, all of their "noticing" will probably be on an unconscious level. The unconscious mind is acutely aware of these subtle cues, a remnant from our evolution as mammals and social animals, even when the conscious mind is otherwise occupied.

The greater the extent to which you can pace and match these subtleties of speech, the more in sync your listener(s) will believe you are with them. Out of this sense of synchronicity and under-standing comes a sense of rapport, the first key element to effective communication.

LEADING

After you've paced a person for a while, you may want to try leading them. Make small changes in your language, body posture, rate of speech, or even speed of breathing. If they're really feeling in sync with you, they'll unconsciously follow your changes. When you see that happen, you know that they're in a highly receptive state and will attend carefully to your communications.

This is a strategy that good public speakers use, whether they realize it or not. They start out with a pace, tempo, cadence, tone, and vocabulary that's as baseline or common-denominator as pos-sible. From there they escalate to progressively stronger and more intense states of emotion and insight, using their body language, tone of voice, speed of speech, and complexity of language to bring their audience along with them.

As with any tools, communication tools like this are most use-ful if you practice with them until you're comfortable using them. The more effectively you can attend to the people around you, catch-ing the nuances of their speech, posture, language, and so on, the more quickly you can "enter their world" and help them to enter your world by leading them.

WORKING WITH CHILDREN

Pacing and leading children may seem as if an adult would have to act like a child in order to step into their world. In fact, your matching, pacing, and leading can be much more subtle. Speaking at the same speed is useful, and trying to—in your own and natural way—mirror their emotional state is a good way of beginning. But instead of behaving in a childlike way, you're expressing the adult version of the child's state. This way it feels natural to both you and the child, and your modeling the child's world in an adult way can also provide a good role model for, "This is what it looks like when you grow up."

When I was the executive director of the Children's Village in New Hampshire, one of the kids in our care fell off a horse and split her lip open on the ground. She was crying loudly.

My first instinct was to try to calm her down, but I also knew that this was an instinct that arose from my own personal and internal sense of alarm at another person's being in pain and came out of *my* needs, not *hers*. She needed somebody to step into her world and then lead her out of it.

So instead of saying, "Everything will be OK," or "Don't cry," I ran over to her and said, "Wow, I'll bet that really hurts!" She looked up, stopped crying almost immediately, and through hiccupping sobs said, "Yeah, it does!"

"It always hurts a lot when you first injure yourself," I said. "And you're bleeding too. That probably hurt the most when you first hit the ground." (Notice the presupposition here: by talking about the *past*—when she hit the ground—I'm helping her unconscious mind begin the process of putting the hurt into the past. The statement really said, "At one time it hurt more than it does now.")

"It did!" she said, sitting up, wiping the blood on the back of her arm.

"You've cut yourself before, or skinned your knee and it's bled, right?"

"Yeah," she said.

"And then the bleeding stopped?"

"Yeah, then I get a scab."

"I wonder how many minutes it'll take for your lip to stop

bleeding and for it to stop hurting?" I said, noticing that the bleeding had already mostly stopped.

She touched herself gently and said, "It seems like it's stopping now."

Notice here what had happened up to this point—I'd stepped into her world of pain and then moved her attention from the pain to the healing. I helped her remember times when she'd been injured and had healed, and I'd even helped her to point out to herself that it *always* happened that way. Now for the final step.

"I wonder if you're strong enough to get back on the horse again now?" I said. (She was a girl who valued her own strength: if her main value had been pride or bravery or something else, I would have used that word instead of "strong enough.")

She stood up and dusted herself off, looking at the horse with a smile. "I can do it now."

"Are you sure?" I said, using a tonality that implied I *knew* she could do it. "I know you're strong, and it looks to me like your lip is much better now. But are you strong enough to get back up on that horse?"

"Just watch," she said, flipping herself back up into the saddle.

TALKING CIRCLES

I've had the privilege to spend time on several Native American reservations, as well as both attending and speaking at a major conference on Native American spirituality and wellness. One of the Native American rituals I've participated in numerous times is something called the *Talking Circle,* and my experience in both participating in it and using it with groups of people is that it can be a strong healing agent and skill builder for people with ADHD. It can be used among friends, in school situations, and particularly in families and support groups.

In Native tribes from the Apache to the Hopi (which is a pretty huge cultural chasm), I've noticed something quite different from the way people communicate in White cultures. Conversation in White (and even Black and Hispanic—really, to generalize, I should probably say "mainstream American") cultures is often a competitive sport. If there are several people together, the strongest conversational competitor will win out, dominating the conversation and often the group; the weakest may not be heard from at all.

Native American culture values cooperation over competition, and this is reflected in virtually every aspect of their lives and lifestyles. Many of the Native Americans I've met engage in conversation quite differently from the "American competitive style": they listen, usually looking down and not establishing eye contact, until the person speaking is completely finished. Then they talk, and they fully expect to be able to completely finish their thought before they're interrupted or the conversation goes off to another person.

This style of conversation is fully expressed in the Talking Circle. In this conversational situation, a sacred object, such as a carved stick, feather, or something else meaningful, is passed around the circle in a clockwise direction.

These are the "rules" for the Talking Circles I've been a part of:

1. The person holding the object is the only one with the right to speak, even if they take a long time to think about what to say and there's a pause in the conversation.
2. If somebody else in the circle wants to comment on what's being said, those comments are limited to noises that can be made through the nose, usually just a soft grunt of agreement. Negative comments are strongly discouraged or outright banned. Otherwise, each person must wait their turn.

3. When the object comes to you, you may talk about "whatever is in your heart." In other words, while there may be an overall topic that the Talking Circle is centered around, conversation is by no means limited to this. A person is absolutely free to say whatever is in their heart, without limitation, and in the safe and comfortable knowledge that nobody will criticize it or interrupt it.

4. If a person talks overly long, people around the circle begin to discreetly cough. "Overlong" is usually defined according to the situation but could be three minutes to ten minutes, depending on the size of the group, the topic, and how long the group wants to spend together. If you have the object and notice that others are coughing, it's time to pass it along. (Use of a timer or gong would be highly inappropriate for a Talking Circle, as it's an artificial imposition on the organic process of the Circle.)

5. The circle goes around and around, either until everybody has had one opportunity to talk (usually in a larger group with time constraints) or until each person, when they receive the object, expresses the feeling that they've pretty much said everything they have to say. It's interesting to see how this works: the process is usually quite organic, and everybody pretty much "winds down" about the same time.

Talking Circles are cathartic, healing, and extraordinarily effective ways of bringing everybody into the process of communication and group life. Because you can't speak until you have the object, the skills of listening carefully and learning how to remember what you want to say when your time comes are developed and exercised.

I've seen Talking Circles have a powerful impact on groups of ADHD adults and children, and in our family we often do them, even inviting friends over to do them as if they were a parlor game. ("Come on over to our house for dinner and a one-hour Talking Circle!") I highly recommend you try one out a few times with your friends, family, or even your ADHD support group, if you belong to one.

PART 5

Reinventing Your Life

19

Making Intentional Decisions about Friendships

If a man does not make new acquaintance as he advances through life, he will soon find himself left alone. A man, Sir, should keep his friendship in constant repair.

SAMUEL JOHNSON (1709–1784), BRITISH WRITER,
RECORDED BY JAMES BOSWELL FOR *THE LIFE OF
SAMUEL JOHNSON*, 1755 (PUBLISHED IN 1791)

RELATIONSHIPS ARE AMONG the most important things in life and one of the most problematic areas for children with ADHD. Parents of ADHD kids are often dismayed to discover that their kids will naturally fall in with other high-energy and often problem-behavior children and are looking for a way to change that pattern. Remember the test you took in chapter 1 and the discussion that we often seek friends who share a common way of perceiving the world? Also, ADHDers may relate more intensely—or, on the other hand, have more difficulty relating to others—so this is doubly important to them.

Thirty or more years ago, *USA Today* ran an article about social research that had found that a child's peers exerted 500 percent more influence on the child's values and behavior than did their parents. At first, I couldn't believe this, but the more I looked at my own life and those of others I knew, the more it made sense. Of course, our parents instill in us the baseline values, the core concepts of right and wrong, what our goals and self-worth are, and the other million details that make up our baseline personality. But it's our friends, more often than not, who lead us in one direction or another.

Realizing this, Louise and I decided as parents that instead of trying to micromanage our children's behaviors, we'd work on managing who their friends were. If you're the parent of an ADHD child, this can help you help your child navigate friendships that you think already are or may become problematic. Of course, you can't say, "You may only play with this child and not with that one," but it is possible to say, "If you play with Bobby, we'll drive you wherever you want and pay your way into movies and give you spending money for the mall, but if you choose instead to play with Billy, we'll do none of those things for you." This strategy seemed to work quite well, and we ended up doing it with all three of our children.

CHOOSING FRIENDS AND ACQUAINTANCES

Given the very high level of influence friends and acquaintances have on us, one of the most important types of decisions we make in our lives is deciding who will be our friends and who will not. Few people do this intentionally or consciously but simply fall in with people in their immediate work, home, or local environment. Children are especially prone to making friends in this way; they go with the flow and don't always consciously choose whom to befriend. You can help them become more conscious of and intentional about this behavior early. Most people never even consider the possibility that they have been making choices—albeit unthinking ones—about their friends and acquaintances all their lives . . . and that those choices are having powerful impacts on practically every facet of their lives right to this moment.

Bringing this choice process to conscious awareness is not Machiavellian or manipulative: it's part of the process of taking control of your life. Most people pay relatively close attention to the food they take into their bodies, whether for reasons of taste or health or both. They have definite preferences, and they pursue them several times daily. So why not have a similar deliberative process for the "thought food" and "psychic food" we take into our body daily as a result of the people we associate with?

Andrew Carnegie came to America around the turn of the century from his native Scotland with just a few dollars in his pocket. During his lifetime, he amassed what was then one of the world's largest fortunes, starting U.S. Steel Company and others, and endowing New York's Carnegie Hall. On his tombstone he specified an epitaph that asserted that he owed his success exclusively to his having been successful in surrounding himself with people smarter than he was.

Carnegie was by no means the first. The phrase, "It's not what you know, but who you know" is such a well-known cliché because it so often is true. Businesspeople know well that the success or failure of a company is more often related to the quality of the people in the organization than to its product or service. Why should it be any different in personal affairs?

20

Discover Your Purpose

ADHD Can Be Your Greatest Gift

Life is measured by the rapidity of change, the succession of influences that modify the being.

GEORGE ELIOT (1819–80), BRITISH WRITER,
FELIX HOLT, THE RADICAL, 1866

A LARGE PART OF HEALING from the experience of growing up as a square peg in a round hole is to find the square hole in which we can fit. Most often, people don't make intentional choices about their jobs or even their mates: they take what comes along. Unfortunately, what comes along is often not the best thing for us.

Few people give truly serious thought to how they're going to spend the rest of their lives. Many people see what happens in their lives as "fate." The notion that what happens is what was supposed to happen overlooks (or excuses) the fact that what happens—even when it happens as the result of seemingly passive behaviors—is really the result of some decision somebody made somewhere at some time. To decide not to decide is a decision! So the idea of "fate" that so many people use as a justification for their failure to plan, organize, or set goals is, at best, logically flawed, and at worst at odds with the highest goals of the very religions that are most often (inaccurately, in my humble opinion) cited as the source of fate. There are many situations, of course, where it's most appropriate to live with our decisions, even if they weren't undertaken with due deliberation and thought. Staying with one's spouse and/or children is a good example. Usually with a little work such situations can be repaired or rebuilt—reinvented—and grow into an important source of nurturing and strength.

But now that you're ready to re-create your life and way of living, it's time to take a look at how you're spending every moment of every day to look for congruence or incongruence with your purpose and goals. While looking ahead and moving forward, prepare to leave behind those people, jobs, habits, and other elements of your life that are counterproductive. With jobs, living spaces, and friendships, it's often very useful to sit down and carefully examine your situation and circumstances for congruence with your purpose and goals.

Taking whatever comes along as a "job" and following it, hoping it'll lead to better things or at least not end up in a layoff, is not a goal. Keeping an eye out for opportunities and "moving up in the world" is probably about as close to a statement of mission or goal as some people have ever said out loud to themselves or anybody else. This is as true for children as it is for adults, whether it has to do with their school goals or their life goals.

Sometimes people will become sufficiently motivated to create goals for themselves. Often these are stated in vague terms, such as, "Make more money," or "Have a better job." Sometimes they're even quite specific: "Become the manager of this business," or "Earn $60,000 per year within two years." There have been many books written and speeches given in the field of self-improvement about goal setting and its importance. Having a goal is, of course, the first step to achieving a goal.

The problem with many of these books and techniques is that they overlook the larger implications of the goal itself. What happens when you reach it? What's next after that? And will reaching the first or subsequent goals really make you happy? Goals in a vacuum are no more useful than putting on a winter coat without knowing what season it is or what the temperature outside is.

Goals should exist within a larger and more important context: *purpose*.

When you consider your purpose before jumping into a job, you're likely to hunt for and find a position that is long-lasting and gives your life meaning and joy. There are many jobs, life situations, and relationships that well suit individuals with ADHD, just as there are many that don't. Just as alcoholics are well advised to avoid going into bars, Hunters should avoid situations and places that will badly and repeatedly stress their attention spans. If you currently make a living as a bookkeeper, for example, you may want to consider shifting into sales of bookkeeping services instead. Find a niche where you fit and are comfortable and happy.

Few people ever give any thought at all to their purpose.

People with ADHD are often so whipsawed by growing up as Hunters in a Farmer's world that they don't have or take the time to consider their futures.

Accept for a moment, just for the sake of discussion, that there is some *reason* you're here on this planet at this time. That being the case, what do you think that reason is? Imagine, for a moment, yourself before your birth, a disembodied spirit, looking down on your parents a few days before you were conceived, thinking about why you're choosing to slide down into that new body they're going to prepare for you. What will you be doing? What will make you happy? How will you serve others? *What is your purpose?*

Purpose is often easy to identify, even if you've never considered the question for more than a few seconds. If you think of the answers to the following questions, you'll have a good sense/vision/sound of your purpose:

- What have been my most fulfilling moments?
- In my most secret fantasies about my life, what do I see myself doing?
- What are the things I've done in my life that have given me the greatest—and most lasting—pleasure?
- Who are my heroes, and how and why do they seem heroic to me? In what ways do I know that if I were to emulate them, I would be fulfilling my purpose?

It's easy to mistake an aspect of purpose for purpose itself. Many people get off on this sidetrack and remain there their entire lives.

To give you a personal example, when I was a child, I had a good friend two years older than I was whose father was a stage magician. I thought that was really cool, and Chuck and I both became magicians, performing at parties and even on local television. When I was twelve, I joined the local magicians' guild as a professional. I thought my purpose was to be an entertainer. However, when I was fourteen, I earned a summer scholarship to Michigan State University's biochemistry program, and to this day I vividly remember presenting my paper at the end of that term to a group of assembled parents and instructors. It was such a rush, telling them about my findings of how the drug colchicine had produced microscopic spore-pod mutations in *Aspergillus* and *Rhizopus*. I interpreted that as more proof that I should entertain people, be on stage as it were. During college, I got a job in a local radio station as a disc jockey and then went into radio news, where I worked part-time for seven years. It was fun, but it also didn't seem all that fulfilling. It wasn't until I was ordained and took over a small church in Detroit that I realized that it wasn't entertaining people that really turned me on, but teaching them.* I was born a

---

*The story of this part of my life is told in detail in my book *The Prophet's Way* (Mythical Books, 1996).

teacher: that is a very large part of my purpose. I continue to teach as often as possible, both in person and through my writing. It's so important to me that I don't charge local groups a fee to give speeches on ADHD or other topics of importance to me: that's my *purpose*. It took me a while to discover it, but looking back on my life I can see how crystal clear it was even from my earliest childhood memories.

You have a similar clear sense of your purpose, if only you'll look or listen. Somewhere in there, if you examine your life, memories, joys, boredoms, and high- and low-points, you'll find a common thread. Someplace there was or is something that clicks. That's where you'll find the signposts to your true purpose.

Once you've determined your purpose, *then* it's time to set goals.

The most important part of goal setting is to visualize clear goals. Where most people fail in this regard is that they don't properly adjust the submodalities of their visualized goals. (I don't know of a single book that discusses this method, drawn from NLP.)

For example, bring up a picture of something that you absolutely know you are going to do in the next few days. Look at the picture. Notice its modalities—does it have sound? Feelings? Smells or tastes? What about the submodalities—is it in color? Movie or still? Associated or disassociated? Where in space is it located around you? How clear is it? Check out all the submodalities and make a mental catalog.

Now pull up the picture of a goal you have set for yourself and check out its modalities and submodalities. Odds are, they're qualitatively different—indicating that what you've pulled up is a *wish* and not a *goal*.

Check out that goal picture for the feelings associated with it. Is it congruent with your purpose? Do you feel excited by it? Ask yourself if there are other parts of you that would rather you didn't reach that goal, and if you get affirmative responses, ask those parts what they're trying to accomplish and what they object to. Walk them through the centering exercise from earlier in this book.

When you have congruence with all your parts about that future goal, when you're quite sure that it's something you want to achieve, then pull the picture up again and begin, one by one, to adjust the submodalities of your picture so that they're identical qualitatively to the submodalities of your "certain I'm going to do it" picture. When you have it totally tweaked so that it's identical in all respects, notice how you feel about it. If you still feel good about it and no parts are objecting, odds are that there's now a certainty and power associated with your visualization, which it previously lacked.

If you do this properly, you'll discover over the next few weeks that you're drawn to do those things that will further your goal and reject or avoid those things that will take you away from it. It's no longer a struggle. It becomes automatic.

Goethe, the German author of *Faust,* noted this when he wrote, "Until one is committed, there is hesitancy, the chance to draw back, always ineffectiveness. . . . The moment one commits oneself, then providence moves too. All sorts of things occur to help one that would otherwise never have happened. A whole stream of events issues from the decision, raising in one's favor all manner of unforeseen incidents and meetings and material assistance, which no man could have dreamed would come his way."

The key here is *committed.* While most people will say, "Yes, I am committed to that goal," what they have not done is adjust their visualization of the goal so that the submodalities are consistent with those they create when they're committed. By adjusting those submodalities, the mental image of the goal is moved from the "maybe" part of the brain to the "definitely going to happen" area. And so it happens!

WORKING WITH CHILDREN

A study published in the October 1992 issue of *Journal of Learning Disabilities* found that people with ADHD and other "learning disabilities" who'd grown up to be successful or highly successful adults had two primary things in common with each other. The first was that they'd "reframed" their experience of the learning disability, coming to see it as either a difference or even a gift instead of as a "deficit." The first third of this book is about that. The second big difference between unsuccessful and successful people was that the successful ones had learned, presumably when they were children, how to visualize their goals and then reach for those goals.

The processes described in this chapter are laid out in the context of an adult, but they work just as well for children. Every year around Christmastime, we have sat down with our children and helped them write down their goals both for the coming year and for their lives. We've helped walk them through the exercise of determining their purpose. And then we had them thumbtack that piece of paper to the inside of their closet, where they'd see it every day when getting dressed.

This process works very well with children, and there is virtually no minimum age: if the child is old enough to understand the concept of goal setting and future (usually around four to six), they are old enough to begin learning how to set goals, visualize them, and then work toward them. It's perfectly okay if the goals change—even if they change weekly—just so long as the process is done and the skills are learned. As children who learned these skills grow up, even when they're "afflicted" with ADHD, the skills will become a part of their normal lives and help them to succeed in the world.

• ● •

Thinking of living on the edge of change like this is often uncomfortable. If you reframe it, however, in the context of taking the steps to move toward a more pleasurable and fulfilling future, you may find that the discomfort dissipates, replaced by excitement and anticipation. What will you learn from that new job and from those new friends? How will you grow and expand your emotional, spiritual, and personal power? How can you help the world and those who live in it?

21

Re-create Your
Environment Intentionally

*To affect the quality of the day, that is the highest of
arts. Every man is tasked to make his life, even in its
details, worthy of the contemplation of his most elevated
and critical hour.*

HENRY DAVID THOREAU (1817–1862),
AMERICAN WRITER, *WALDEN*, 1854

A FINAL STEP IN HEALING from society's reaction to ADHD and
reinventing your life is to re-create the space you live in.

For some people, a good anchor is very important in doing
this, and it may be particularly helpful for people with ADHD.
Specifically, anchors may help you focus your intention or mood in a
certain space, and in so doing help you create new habits. In the lit-
erary world, stories abound about writers who could "only" write on
their old 1947 Underwood or other writers who had to have a new
typewriter or computer for every book they wrote. It's not uncom-
mon for couples going through a lot of change and transformation
in their personal lives to redecorate their house, bedroom, or even
buy an entire new home. Those anchors that are most powerfully
connected with seeking-pleasure motivation strategies tend to be

the ones we want to keep around, whereas those connected with avoiding-pain strategies are the ones that are most often recycled.

CREATING SPECIFIC SPACES

Now that you understand that virtually everything in your living space is an anchor for some particular feeling or state of mind, you can make a step-by-step evaluation of everything around you. Do you want to keep it as it is, change it, discard it, or replace it?

The recent rediscovery and growing popularity of the ancient twin art/sciences of Feng Shui and Geomancy help modern people to recognize the importance of set and setting. Not only is arranging important for proper energy, but the very act of rearranging helps to break up old anchors and gives an opportunity to install new ones from a positive and hopeful mind-set.

When creating new spaces or reinventing old ones, be intentional. Decide what feelings you want associated with a space and bring them to the fore while first sitting/standing/being in that place. Repeat the exercise a few times. Say a prayer that the site will be invested with the particular energy or essence you want to experience in it.

If there is some new habit you want to begin, such as daily prayer or meditation or reading, then designate a place for that and only use it for your new activity. Isolate the most destructive things in the house (such as the TV) to places that are relatively uncomfortable, so they'll only be used when absolutely necessary.

THINGS AS ANCHORS

Your clothes are anchors too. Each outfit or component lends a certain feeling or mood to you and your day, and consciously noticing this gives you an edge in deciding in the morning what sort of day you're going to make. Often this is a self-fulfilling prophecy, but that makes it no less real. I remember forty years ago reading in the then-new book *Dress for Success* that dark pinstripe suits were "power suits." Whenever I was going into a business meeting where I'd be negotiating or doing something where I thought it would be useful to be perceived as powerful, I'd wear a dark blue pinstripe suit. It became such an anchor for me that to this day, when I put on such a suit, I find myself standing more erect and breathing more deeply.

In ancient times, people carried with them charms or fetishes that were carved images of one of their gods or were believed to conduct the power of a particular spirit to them. In the burial sites of ancient peoples (two thousand to nine thousand years old) in Europe and the Americas, archaeologists have often found such objects, along with presumably sacred stones or bits of ornamental wood, bone, or shell. In modern times, people use jewelry, money clips, lucky coins, key rings, or particular types of minerals to bring them good luck or conduct particular types of vibrations into or around them. Some athletes will only wear a particular jersey or glove, convinced that it gives them power to win a game. While these may carry the properties advertised, they're also powerful anchors for particular states and, as such, should be treated with respect.

On the other hand, it's also important to recognize fetishes and charms for what they usually are—simply anchors, whose meaning we are free to choose for ourselves. Many people don't realize they have this power of choice and suffer greatly for it. For example, in 1899, Sigmund Freud had a new phone number assigned to him by the Vienna telephone company. The number—14362—so alarmed Freud that he began having nightmares. Because he was then forty-three years old, he believed that the two numbers surrounding his current age—the 1 and 6 on either side of the 43—were omens of the age he'd attain when he would die. He spent the next eighteen years morbidly obsessing on his preparations to die at the age of sixty-one. It turned out to be an unnecessary waste of time: he finally left this world when, wracked by a painful cancer, he committed suicide (with the help of a physician friend) at the age of eighty-three.

The moral of Freud's story is that when we understand how anchors work, we can choose to use them or discard them. You can create sacred places in and around your house, have power clothes and healing crystals or jewelry, and define happy and fighting locations for your interactions with your spouse or coworkers—but all consciously, with specific intent.

REGAINING CONTROL OF YOUR LIFE

The summary of all of these techniques and strategies to redefine, re-create, reempower, recover, and heal is that it's not only possible to heal from the wounds and discomforts of growing up as a Hunter in a Farmer's world, but that it can even be fun. With the tools in this book, you can take control of your life and teach your children to do the same for themselves. You can recalibrate your and their way of responding to the world. You can choose how you want to remember your past and how you want it to affect you. You can choose how to live in the present. And you can invent a new future for yourself and your children.

And you can do it all now.

Bibliography

Andreas, Connierae, and Tamara Andreas. *Core Transformation*. Moab, Utah: Real People Press, 1994.

Armstrong, Thomas. *The Myth of the ADD Child: 101 Ways to Improve Your Child's Behavior and Attention Span Without Drugs, Labels, or Coercion*. New York: Tarcher, 2017.

Bandler, Richard, and John Grinder. *The Structure of Magic: A Book About Language and Therapy*. Palo Alto, Calif.: Science and Behavior Books, 1975.

Barker, Eric. "Wondering What Happened to Your Class Valedictorian? Not Much, Research Shows." *Money,* May 18, 2017. Reprinted from Barker's book *Barking Up the Wrong Tree: The Surprising Science behind Why Everything You Know About Success Is (Mostly) Wrong*. New York: HarperCollins, 2017.

Brown, Kristen V. "How Posture Influences Mood, Energy, Thoughts." SFGate website, September 3, 2013.

Bunzel, B., B. Schmidl-Mohl, and G. Wollenek. "Does Changing the Heart Mean Changing the Personality? A Retrospective Inquiry on 47 Heart Transplant Patients." *Quality of Life Research* 1 no. 4 (1992): 251–56.

Fehmi, Les. Open Focus website.

Gerber, Paul J., Rick Ginsberg, and Henry B. Reiff. "Identifying Alterable Patterns in Employment Success for Highly Successful Adults with

Learning Disabilities." *Journal of Learning Disabilities* 25 no. 8 (October 1992): 475–87.

Goleman, Daniel. *Emotional Intelligence: Why It Can Matter More than IQ.* New York: Bantam, 1995.

Hallowell, Edward, and John J. Ratey. *Driven to Distraction: Recognizing and Coping with Attention Deficit Disorder from Childhood through Adulthood.* New York: Simon & Schuster, 1995.

Kaminer, Wendy. *I'm Dysfunctional, You're Dysfunctional.* New York: Vintage, 1993.

Levy, Raymond, and Victor Meyer. "Ritual Prevention in Obsessional Patients." *New Techniques in Behaviour Therapy* 64 (November 1971): 1115–8.

Lorayne, Harry, and Jerry Lucas. *The Memory Book.* London: W. H. Allen, 1975.

Lowe, G. "Alcohol and State-Dependent Learning." *Substance & Alcohol Actions/Misuse.* 4 no. 4 (1983): 273–82.

Lowth, Marcus. "10 Organ Recipients Who Took On The Traits of Their Donors." Listverse website. May 14, 2016.

Moses, Lucia. "A Look at Kids' Exposure to Ads: Children See a Lot of Marketing Messages, Regardless of Platform." *Adweek* website. March 11, 2014.

Science News Staff. "Extra Licking Makes for Relaxed Rats," *Science* website, September 11, 1997.

Volk, Steve. "Rewiring the Brain to Treat OCD. A Groundbreaking Therapy, Relying on Mindfulness Meditation to Treat Obsessive Compulsive Disorder, Suggests Even Adult Brains Have Neuroplasticity." *Discover Magazine* website, December 11, 2013.

Weiss, Lynn. *A.D.D. and Creativity.* Dallas: Taylor, 1997.

Wolin, Steven, and Sybil Wolin, *The Resilient Self: How Survivors of Troubled Families Rise Above Adversity.* New York: Villard, 1993.

Index

abnormal, 26–27

abuse, 47

accommodations, 31

acetylcholine, 47

A.D.D. and Creativity (Weiss), 73

ADD Success Stories (Hartmann), 45

ADHD

  better definitions, 26–27

  damage from growing up with, 54–60

  friends and, 156–58

  as greatest gift, 159–66

  healing of, 29–32

  issues with labeling, 11–12

  label of, 4–5

  needs of society and, 71–73

  possible explanations of, 46–53

  as response to modern world, 67–73

  stigmatization of, 62–66

  wounding and, 28–29

ADHD: A Hunter in a Farmer's World (Hartmann), 47, 52

advertising, 5, 18

alcoholics, 77–78

aliveness, 52

alpha waves, 120

American Psychiatric Association, 15, 50

anchors, 132–37, 167–70

Andreas, Connierae, 89

Andreas, Tamara, 89

anger, 20

antidepressants, 27

antipsychotics, 123

anxiety, 25–26

anxiety disorders, 104

Apache, 151

apostates, 13

Aristotle, 13–14, 15, 141

Arkwright, Richard, 64

Armstrong, Thomas, 49

assumptions, 34

attentional freedom, 119–22
attentional ossification, 116–17
auditory, 6, 93, 118–19
Australia, 72–73
average students, 57
avoiding-pain mechanism, 127

Bandler, Richard, 5, 44, 104, 117,
    130, 144
Baxter, Lewis, 109
BBC (British Broadcasting
    Corporation), 65
Beatles, the, 39
bed, 136
behaviors, 43–45, 80
beliefs, 34–35
    change in, 43–45
    limiting beliefs, 36–37
    modeling other people's, 42–43
big business, 18, 23, 25, 65
Bill (case story), 12–13
Black Ships, 72
blame, 29
blue-green algae, 46
body as a machine, 46
bounties, 19
brain disease, 46–47
brain scans, 109–10
brain surgery, 12
Broca's area, 139
Bush, George, 98

calm center, 79–81, 89
Carnegie, Andrew, 158
carousel music, 115

categories, 13–17
Catholic Church, 13, 84
center, 79–81
Charles V, King, 63
childhood, 76–78
children, 96–97, 148–50, 165
Churchill, Winston, 25–26, 43
Civilization and Its Discontents
    (Freud), 30
classifying, 14
clothing, 168–69
commitment, 164
communications, 5
communication skills, 143–53
complaining, 86–91
concatenating negatives, 137–38
confusion, 1–2
consciousness, 85
conservative, 24
control panel, 94, 97
Copernicus, Nicolaus, 14
core, 89
corporations, 23, 25, 65
courage, 31
cranks, 23
creativity, 73
critical submodality, 95–96
criticisms, 28
cultists, 23
culture, 15, 17–20

damage, 54–60
Darwin, Charles, 16
death penalty, 20
defective, 35

Democrats, 24

depression, 26–27

Descartes, René, 14

devils, 13

diabetes, 22

Diagnostic and Statistical Manual (DSM), 50

discomfort, 32

disconnection, 27

diseased, 35

disempowerment, 29

disinhibition, 51–53

disordered, 35

disorganization, 28

distractibility, 28, 48, 49–50

dopamine, 47

Dress for Success, 169

Driven to Distraction (Hallowell and Ratey), 50

drug companies, 49

drugs, 31

drunk driving, 20

Dukakis, Michael, 98

dysfunctional parts, 81–82

eccentrics, 18

Edison, Thomas, 26

EEG Neurofeedback, 120

Eisenhower, Dwight D., 23

electricity, 14, 26

electroshock treatments, 12

Emotional Intelligence (Goleman), 56

empowered states, 101–4

enlightenment, 80

environment, re-creating, 167–70

Erickson, Milton, 38, 44, 85–86

ethnic cleansing, 16

exercise, lack of, 47

Exposure, Response, and Prevention (ERP), 109–10

eyes, 101–4

families, 17

Farish, William, 56

Farmers, 59

fatalism, 128

fate, 159–60

Faust (Goethe), 164

fear, 25–26, 100

feeling, 5, 92, 121

Fehmi, Les, 120

Feingold, Benjamin, 47

floating, 116

Ford, Henry, 16

Franklin, Benjamin, 16, 18, 26, 43, 65

freethinkers, 22, 64

Freud, Sigmund, 30, 82–85, 169

friends, 5–6

friendships, 156–58

Fromm-Reichmann, Frieda, 25–26

frontal lobes, 47, 108

future, 98–99, 108, 110–12

future access, 132–37

gangs, 20

Gestapo, 25–26

goals, 126, 160–64

Goebbels, Joseph, 22

Goethe, Johann, 164

Goldwater, Barry, 24
Goleman, Daniel, 56
"good," definitions of, 18–19
government, 18, 23, 25
Grinder, John, 5, 44, 104, 144
grist, 1
gustatory, 93
Guthrie, Woody, 40

Hallowell, Edward, 12, 50
happiness, 27
Hartmann Modality-Preference
    Measurement Index, 6–10
Hawaii, 77
hearing, 92, 121
heart disease, 22
heretics, 13
hierarchy, 17–20
Hitler, Adolf, 16–17, 21–24
Hopi, 151
Horton, Willy, 98
Hunters, 30, 59
hunting-gathering world, 30
Huxley, Thomas, 16
hyperactivity, 49–50

I'm Dysfunctional, You're
    Dysfunctional (Kaminer), 77–78
impulsivity, 48, 49–50
independents, 64
Industrial Revolution, 64
inhibition, 51–53
insomnia, 130
interactive sensory flexibility,
    118–19

internal tonality, 130
interruption, 86–91
isolation, 58–60

James, William, 103
Japan, 71–72
Jefferson, Thomas, 16, 18, 56
Journal of Learning Disabilities,
    165
joy, 27
judgments, 28

Kaminer, Wendy, 77–78
Kennedy, John, 43
killing, 19
kinesthetic, 6, 93

labels, 31, 35, 55
lead, 47
leading as communication skill,
    148
learning disabilities, 139–42
learning skills, 139–42
left-handedness, 13, 28
Lennon, John, 37, 42
liberal, 24
light bulbs, 26
Limbaugh, Rush, 49
limiting beliefs, 36–37
Lincoln, Abraham, 16
Lindbergh, Charles, 16
location, 96
Lorayne, Harry, 141
love, 89
Luddites, 23

Madison, James, 18
Maslow, Abraham, 31, 52
Masterpiece Theatre, 68
matching, 143–48
meditation, 132–33
Meiji Era, 71–72
Mein Kampf (Hitler), 21–24
memory and memories, 83–84
  empowered states and, 101–4
  reconstructing the past, 92–97
mental weakness, 28
messiness, 28
Meyer, Victor, 109
milk allergies, 47
modalities, 92–96
modern world, 67–73
moral weakness, 28
motivation, 123–29, 135
movies, 115
MRI scan, 12
multiple personality disorder
  (MPD), 81
murder, 58

naming, 14
Native Americans, 16, 17–18, 19,
  150–53
natural communication, 143–44
nature, 85
Nazis, 22
needs, 80
negative feelings, 27
negatives, processing, 137–38
negativity, 128
neurofeedback, 120

Neuro-Linguistic Programming
  (NLP), 1–2, 5, 101–4
neuroses, 76–77, 82, 84–85
neurotransmitters, 47, 85, 109
nirvana, 80
Nixon, Richard, 23
noncomformity, 19
noncompliance, 19
"normal," 2, 19–20, 25–26
"not good," ADHD as, 18–19
novelty, 48
novelty-seeking behavior, 52, 71–73
nutrition, 47

obesity, 22
observe time, 121
obsessive-complulsive disorder
  (OCD), 109–10
occipital lobes, 47
oddballs, 18
Ohm's Law, 14
olfactory, 93
Olympics, 22–23
organization of humanity, 15–16
overeating, 86

pacing, 143–48
pain, 32, 125–26
paralysis, 82–83
parenting, 47, 54–55, 65
parietal lobes, 47
particles, 14
parts, 80–91, 81–91, 129–30
past, 108, 111–14
Pavlov, Ivan, 133

people, differences between, 4–5
perception, 33–34
personality, 82
personal power, 31
pesticides, 47
PET scan, 12
phobias, 100, 104–6
Picasso, Pablo, 37
pictures, 115
Plato, 5
pleasure, 125–26
positive states, 132–37
posture changes, 135
powerful center, 79–81
procrastination, 129–31
Proverbs, 5, 54
Prozac, 27
psychology, 5, 25–26
Psychology Today, 77–78
psychotherapy, 5, 25–26, 31
public schools, 25–26
purpose, 159–66

racial cleansing, 16
radio, 22
Ralph (story), 36–42
Ratey, John J., 50
reality, 5, 34–36, 93–95
rebellion, 18
rebels, 22
reframing, 10, 31
relationships, 156–58
religion, 84
Representational Systems, 5
Republicans, 24

Resilient Self, The (Wolin and
    Wolin), 77
Richard (case example),
    123–25
risk taking, 48, 49–50
Ritalin, 123

salicylates, 47
salt, 114
samadhi, 80
satori, 80
schools, 68–69
Science News, 67
Scientology, Church of, 49
see, 120
self-actualization, 31
self-esteem, 56–58
self-identity, 35
self-ness, 122
sense space, 121
serotonin, 47, 109
shattering, 115
sight, 5, 92
skills, 31–32
slavery, 15–16
smell, 5, 92, 121
smoking, 86
social hierarchies, 17
sound, 5
special education, 31
SPECT scan, 12
spelling, 141–42
stacking anchors, 134
standardized curriculum, 57
sterilization, 16

stigmatization, 62–66
strength, 76–78
Structure of Magic, The (Bandler), 104
stuckness, 118
subluxations, 47
submodalities, 92–96, 97
success, 25, 56–58
sugar, 47
suicide, 58
sunlight, 47
"system, the," 18

Taiwan, 72–73
Talking Circles, 150–53
taste, 5, 92, 121
television, 18, 22–23
thalamic function, 52
therapy, 78
thinking, 121–22
thought-control device, 22–23
timelines, 108–16
trauma, 83
TV, 47, 68

unhappiness, 26–27
United Kingdom, 123

United States, 18, 72–73
universe-as-a-machine paradigm, 14
USA Today, 156–57

valedictorians, 57
victims, 77
video games, 69
visual, 6, 93, 118–19
visual cortex, 139

Washington, George, 18, 26
Watt, James, 64
weak beliefs, 35
weakness, 28
Weiss, Lynn, 73
Wernicke's area, 139
wheat allergies, 47
Williams, Robin, 23
Wilson, Charles, 19
witches, 13
witness self-ness, 122
Wolin, Steven, 77
Wolin, Sybil, 77
wounding, 28–29

Zappa, Frank, 39

BOOKS OF RELATED INTEREST

Adult ADHD
How to Succeed as a Hunter in a Farmer's World
by Thom Hartmann

ADHD and the Edison Gene
A Drug-Free Approach to Managing the Unique
Qualities of Your Child
by Thom Hartmann

Walking Your Blues Away
How to Heal the Mind and Create Emotional Well-Being
by Thom Hartmann

The Prophet's Way
A Guide to Living in the Now
by Thom Hartmann

The Neurofeedback Solution
How to Treat Autism, ADHD, Anxiety, Brain Injury,
Stroke, PTSD, and More
by Stephen Larsen, Ph.D.

Remapping Your Mind
The Neuroscience of Self-Transformation through Story
by Lewis Mehl-Madrona, M.D., Ph.D.
with Barbara Mainguy, M.A.

Out of Your Comfort Zone
Breaking Boundaries for a Life Beyond Limits
by Emma Mardlin, PhD

Mind Detox
Discover and Resolve the Root Causes of Chronic
Conditions and Persistent Problems
by Sandy C. Newbigging

INNER TRADITIONS • BEAR & COMPANY
P.O. Box 388 • Rochester, VT 05767
1-800-246-8648 • www.InnerTraditions.com

Or contact your local bookseller